The Health Advocate's Start & Grow Your Own Practice Handbook

By
Trisha Torrey,
Every Patient's Advocate

DiagKNOWsis Media

The Health Advocate's Start and Grow Your Own Practice Handbook
A Step-by-Step Guide

CS15

HealthAdvocateResources.com

Trisha Torrey, Every Patient's Advocate
PO Box 53
Baldwinsville, NY 13027
1-888-478-6588
contact@diagKNOWsis.com

Discounts for bulk-orders of this book are available by contacting the author. Trisha Torrey is also available for speaking opportunities to groups of patients or professionals.

DiagKNOWsis Media
PO Box 53
Baldwinsville, NY 13027
www.DiagKNOWsis.com

ISBN: 978-0-9828014-1-3

Printed in the United States of America

Dedication

When I began my journey into the land of patient advocacy, I felt a bit biblical about it... sort of a loaves and fishes thing. Instead of reaching one person at a time through my patient empowerment work, I could instead help one advocate who could, in turn, help dozens, if not hundreds of patients.

What I've learned along the way is that many advocates approach their work with a spirit of generosity - a very sharing group! They have asked questions, volunteered resources and supported efforts to grow health advocacy as a profession. Their input has helped me expand the loaves and fishes concept – helping dozens if not hundreds more advocates who, in turn, will help dozens if not hundreds more patients, too.

I thank them all.

I offer special thanks, too, to those who have helped in this publishing journey. My daughter, Becca Simpkins, and my husband, Butch Kritsberg, who put up with my lousy punctuation, badly formed sentences, and figuring out the pieces of the start-a-business puzzle that were missing or weren't explained well. Thanks, too, to my friends and advisors, Amy Cuykendall and Bill Storie who made sure we stayed on the right side of legal and insurance issues. Further thanks go to two folks who pitched in, but asked to remain anonymous. (You know who you are.)

All in all, as you can see, it's been a team effort to put this information together for you. If you've asked a question, made a suggestion, had a complaint, or found a missing piece—you are part of the team.

And so, team – I dedicate this book to you all, with sincere appreciation for your support.

Trisha

This book is the second in the Health Advocacy Career Series:

Learn more about the series, and find links to purchase the additional books at: http://HealthAdvocateResources.com

Table of Contents
(including Sidebar titles)

Preface

See if any of these scenarios sound familiar to you:

Your Great-Aunt Mildred is either very sick, or chronically ill, or recently passed away – and you have been her advocate. You've helped her get to doctor's appointments, made sure she took her meds properly, sorted through her medical bills, or argued with someone in the doctor's office because you felt like she wasn't being cared for in the manner you expected. You learned a lot – you figured out the system and how to solve problems. Now, with all that experience under your belt, you're thinking you might want to make a career out of providing those kinds of services to others.

Or

You've been working in healthcare for most of your career, perhaps as a nurse, or even a doctor. Maybe you're getting ready to retire but want to keep tabs on the work you enjoy. Even more likely, you're tired of the hassle the system itself has thrown in your way. You love the medical and people aspects, but you hate the insurance, payment, and managed parts that come between you and your patients. You feel too often like you're no longer able to be an advocate for your patients because you're too busy marching to someone else's rules. You believe the solution might be to return your practice to the caring aspects of medicine, where you can spend the time needed to truly help someone get the care he or she deserves.

Or

You've recently come through a difficult medical situation yourself or maybe you're dealing with a chronic disease or condition. You might have established a good partnership with your doctor, researched potential treatments, and helped develop your treatment protocols. Or you battled the system, and despite a good number of hurdles placed squarely in your path, you overcame that adversity. Your navigation has been successful – you've not just survived, but feel empowered and capable of helping others, too. A great catharsis or next step would be a career as an advocate to help others weather their healthcare storms.

Of course, there are other reasons you might be reading this book. But most of the folks I've met who have an interest in patient or health advocacy as a career fit one of those descriptions.

Perhaps not surprisingly, my reason for writing this book fits one of those profiles, too.

In 2004 I experienced a major run-in with the American healthcare system. I've told the story many times, and details are available from other sources. But the bottom line was that I was diagnosed with a rare and terminal form of lymphoma and given only a few months to live. Through my own efforts, and despite some real resistance from my first oncologist, I was able to prove I had no cancer at all. These many years later, I've never had any form of treatment.

Over a period of three months, that journey extracted a serious emotional toll (from which I still, on occasion, suffer some post-traumatic stress.) But I learned two things from the experience that have led me to writing this book for you:

First, that the healthcare system, no matter where you live or what is wrong with you, is not set up to provide best outcomes to its patients. It doesn't mean good outcomes aren't possible, or that we won't get them... But the system is set up to abbreviate and ration our care, to impersonalize it, to automate it to the point that most patients get lost in it.

And let's not forget the big daddy of reasons: money. The American healthcare system is set up to make profits. Other health systems, like those in Canada, Australia or the UK, may not be set up for profit-making, but they are set up to be sure that money is conserved and care is rationed; so that not one extra dollar or pound is spent unless it's necessary – by their definition of necessary.

When my odyssey ended, my bill-of-health was declared clean, and my trust level and bank account were totally empty. My levels of anger and blame were maxed out, and I knew I needed to do something to dissipate them.

Since I believe everything happens for a reason, including my misdiagnosis odyssey, I was left trying to figure out what that reason could possibly be. I did some personal introspection and soul searching. To that point in my life I had had two careers – teaching and marketing – both communications professions. I realized that my skill set would help me tell my story, and perhaps help other patients weather their own healthcare storms.

And so I did.

First, I named myself "Every Patient's Advocate". I focused on writing about being a smart patient, and speaking to patient audiences, building websites and writing books... Within a few years my anger had been replaced by the great joy of knowing I was making a difference in people's lives. My brother-in-law, a pastor, dubbed it "Trisha's calling."

Over time, a theme evolved and the same two questions kept popping up.

"I need this kind of help, or my mother needs that kind of assistance.... Do you know of someone who can help?"

And...

"I had this experience (or that career) and now I would love to work directly with patients to help them. What do I need to know to get started?"

Yes. Each side of the equation was asking about the other. As I learned of the availability of patient advocates in different locations, or with different skill sets, I would make those matches – one at a time - dozens of them over the years.

But frustratingly, I know that only a small fraction of those who needed the help ever found me to ask.

My aha! moment came when I realized that I could use the power and reach of the Internet to make those connections happen. In 2006 I began reaching out to independent advocates to connect and learn. In 2007, I began making those patient-advocate matches one-by-one. Then, in 2009, AdvoConnection.com was launched to support those advocates with their business needs, and to showcase them so patients would find them. Finally, in 2012, the membership side of AdvoConnection was given its own identification: The Alliance of Professional Health Advocates (APHA).

Since the patient-to-advocate matching and advocate business support began, the biggest hurdle has been good-old supply and demand. While the profession of health advocacy is growing, it's not growing nearly fast enough to keep up with the needs of patients. My guesstimate is that in any given month, there are 300 or so patients needing every one available advocate, if only those advocates lived in their geographic area, offering the skills and services needed.

So that's the mission that drives me. Making sure the patients who need help can find the help they need. Building patient and health advocacy as a career. Facilitating and matchmaking. Teaching... supporting.... Cheerleading....

Advocate empowerment. Patient empowerment. Improved outcomes. Healthier careers and healthier patients, too.

One way I fulfill my mission is by writing books, including this one, to help you, someone who has an interest in the possibilities of being a paid, professional, health advocate.

In these pages, I hope you will find useful information to help you establish a patient or health advocacy practice.

Is This Book for You?

If you have interest in a career in patient advocacy, you can benefit from reading this book.

However – be aware that there's no sugar coating here. This is no sales job to encourage you to enter the profession. Becoming an advocate won't be easy because there are not many role models or specific tracks to follow.

There are many kinds of patient advocates – from those who help patients navigate the medical aspects of their care, to medical billing and insurance claims advocates, to mediators, case managers or eldercare professionals, to lawyers who build medical malpractice and workers compensation practices, to doulas or acupuncturists, to patient safety consultants. They are all stepping up to help patients.

Some of these professionals are employed by hospitals. Others are employed by insurance companies. Still others are independent, being hired privately by individuals, or by employers who wish to assist their employees.

This book is focused on those potential advocates who wish to build a private practice and be paid directly by a patient, a caregiver, an employer or someone else who is focused on improving the health or medical status of that one individual.

These are advocates who understand that allegiance is important. A hospital's advocate works for the hospital—meaning that advocate understands that her allegiance must be to the hospital, whose needs take priority over patients'. An insurer's advocate works for the insurer and is beholden to the insurer in the same way.

But a private, independent advocate's allegiance is first and foremost to the patient who has the health or medical system need. Her work is focused only on making things right for her patient-clients.

This is where both the need and the growth are. Patients and their caregivers are in search of help, and are ready to pay for it.

Will you be ready to help them?

Introduction

The concept of patient advocacy has been around for centuries, perhaps even before doctoring was a career. Helping others who had medical challenges weather the storms of diagnosis and treatment (or perhaps even before those disciplines existed) – friends and family would lend a hand – would *advocate* - for those they cared about.

Among the first more formal advocates were people who worked with the many disease-oriented organizations that were founded as long ago as the early 20th century. The American Cancer Society and the March of Dimes both have very early roots as organizations that provided one-on-one advocacy-type assistance from someone external to the hospital and doctor practice institutions of the times. Most often that help came from volunteers who had already weathered the same kinds of health storms as the people they helped.

Beginning in the 1960s, not long after the passage of the then-new Medicare law, and as baby boomers began giving birth in bigger numbers, a group called the National Welfare Rights Organization was established. Its mission was to expand people's rights, in particular the rights of women and children. As its influence spread, and as the social movements of the times expanded (think peace, love, hippies, pot, and big, bright flowers painted on Volkswagen vans), a document called the Patient Bill of Rights was developed.

The first so-titled "patient advocates" worked in hospitals, assisting patients and families who, unlike today, were often resident in those hospitals for extended periods of time. Their focus was to make that hospital stay easier. Their work was, in part, based on the Patient Bill of Rights which by then had been adopted by the American Hospital Association.

Even then, patients were mostly able to get the help they needed from the medical system itself. Most care was provided by "GPs" - general practitioners. Even through the transition from house calls to making appointments to see a doctor, money didn't need to change hands very often. Employers (or governments) covered the cost of healthcare, and the word "prevention" was heard mostly in relation to dental cavities.

Fast Forward to Today

Today there is a huge divide between health care – the actual activity of keeping a body healthy, healing one that isn't, or treating pain and discomfort – and the healthcare system which is comprised of the business of delivering that care – from how appointments are handled, to billing and reimbursements by insurance companies. The system itself can either facilitate the delivery of good healthcare, or can stand in the way of that delivery.

Unfortunately, "stand in the way" is too often the reality. Systemic roadblocks brought about by dysfunction or money-saving regulations may prevent patients from getting the care they need, and providers from delivering that care effectively.

Thus the need for today's newer form of health advocates – people who will go to bat for others who either don't have the knowledge needed to successfully overcome the system's challenges, or who are too sick and debilitated to be able to adequately advocate for themselves.

Why Are Advocates So Necessary?

Almost everyone who accesses the healthcare system for anything beyond a cold or a poison ivy rash needs an advocate. No matter how young or old, no matter how much money they have, or how good their insurance or payment system, no matter male or female, and no matter which country of the world they live in.

Here are some of the reasons health advocates are so necessary today:

Aging Baby Boomers

Nearly 79 million Americans, and four million Canadians count themselves as baby boomers. Born between 1946 and 1964, they are the beneficiaries (and victims) of a system that has kept them alive longer than previous generations, which then allows them to age into more diseases. The 75-year-old who didn't die of his heart attack at the age of 50 has now lived long enough to develop diabetes and prostate cancer. Some estimates say that 17% of people who live to 75 will also live to age 100.

But they can't stay healthy enough to live so long without someone – a health advocate – to help them weather the system.

Growth of Chronic Illness

We know that people are living longer, and recovering from illnesses that might have caused an earlier demise. That also means that more and more patients will develop chronic illnesses, and that they will spend a good portion of their lives dealing with them.

More and more patients are developing diabetes due to poor eating habits and choices, and too little exercise. Heart disease patients are managing their diseases to extend their lives. Many cancers that used to be regarded as death sentences are now managed for decades. When added to the numbers of smokers and the obese, the numbers are staggering.

So who do these patients turn to in order to manage those myriad health challenges? Patient advocates.

Mobile Society

Mom and Dad, in their 80s, live in one corner of the country. Their adult children, who are now being called upon to assist Mom and Dad, live in a different corner of the country. They need someone local to Mom and Dad to be on call, to guide them – a patient advocate.

Further, older brother who hasn't been "home" in five years is trying to take control of decisions being made by his younger sister, Mom's caregiver who lives only a mile from Mom. They argue over paying for Mom's nursing home by selling Mom's house. A lifetime of sibling rivalry means no one is getting what they need.

Who can sort it all out? An advocate-mediator.

Employment

Even when those adult children live nearby, they have careers and job responsibilities. They find it challenging to leave work to escort their elderly parents to doctors' appointments, or to sit by their side in the hospital, sometimes more frequently than they ever did for their own children. They need someone to accompany Mom or Dad when the need arises – a patient advocate.

Not Enough Providers

According to the American Medical Association, there will be a shortage of about 160,000 physicians – primary care and specialists – by 2025. Shortages may also mean the bar will be lowered for entering the profession and keeping skills current. So even when patients do find a doctor to help them, there is a chance that person will not have the excellent skills required. Who will help them get the appointments and care they need? A patient advocate.

The Internet and Information Explosion

The more we individuals learn about our symptoms, illnesses and conditions, the more we want to know. At the same time, more and more research is being done to add to the amount of information individuals and professionals may access. (I make no judgment here as to the quality of that information!) It's as if the more we know, the more we want to know! Since no one person can keep up, individuals will look to health advocates to help them sort it all out.

Healthcare Reform and Redesigned Care Delivery

No matter how savvy a patient is, the new reality that will come about as a result of American healthcare reform will cause confusion. The delivery of care is already changing in ways we have trouble comprehending. We're still wondering where Marcus Welby is while having to juggle medical homes and ACOs. Don't know what medical homes or ACOs are? Point made. Advocates will be called upon to sort out the confusion.

Follow the Money

Most patients don't understand that the care they receive is first, and foremost, dependent on how the system will be paid for that care. The CEO with a golden health insurance policy is getting far more attention and better care than the poor Medicaid recipient with mental health problems.

But is that care really better? One problem with today's healthcare model in the United States is the emphasis on tests and procedures. When doctors do "things" they make more money. So that CEO who has great insurance may be subjected to more "things" than she really needs.

Who will help her sort out those tests and procedures? A patient advocate.

And what about those who aren't getting what they need because their insurance policy doesn't cover everything required to treat them? They'll need an advocate, too.

Too Many Medical Errors

With too few doctors, dealing with too much confusion, seeing more patients in less time (because doctors get paid by the patient, tests and procedures, and not by the time they spend with those patients), it is impossible for any doctor NOT to make mistakes.

If the mistake is prescribing too low a drug dose, a dose which can be increased later, there may be little harm done. But if the mistake is amputating the wrong leg, or not washing hands and therefore transmitting an infection, it can mean quantity or quality of life.

If the mistake that is made is a billing mistake, and a patient goes bankrupt, then who has paid the price? We all have.

And who is the most apt, and prepared, to prevent a mistake to begin with? Yes, of course. A patient advocate.

More Childhood Challenges

Babies who never would have been born a generation ago, are surviving birth at only one or two pounds – then spending a lifetime with health challenges that result from lung or heart problems.

Likewise, babies born to healthy mothers at term, are succumbing to the mistakes mentioned above; from delivery process errors perhaps resulting in cerebral palsy, to acquiring an infection which damages their lungs in the hospital nursery, these babies and their families face a lifetime of healthcare system challenges that are growing more challenging as time goes on.

An advocate who focuses on these kinds of challenges can make an immense difference in the lives of all family members.

The Case for Private, Independent Health Advocacy

So yes, there are many reasons health advocates are so necessary.

But let's be clear here. There are health advocates to be found in lots of places. Unfortunately, not all those advocates have the same goals, nor do they deliver their services the same way, with the same positive outcomes for the patient in mind.

Let's take a look at some of the existing forms of advocacy, and why they may, or may not, be helpful to the patients they serve:

Hospital Patient Advocates

Patient advocates, sometimes called patient representatives, patient liaisons or even ombudsmen, may be found working in hospitals. While they may be helpful to patients or families, their real allegiance must be to their employer – to the hospital. They are usually a part of the Risk Management or Legal Department. Their goal, and their employment, is dependent on keeping the hospital out of hot water, and avoiding lawsuits.

Hospitals also employ "cancer navigators" – a relatively new concept that has become more mainstream in recent years. For someone who has been diagnosed with certain forms of cancer, these navigators can be a godsend. But there are some problems inherent in their employ as well; in some hospitals they are available only to low-income or uninsured patients. In others they work for the hospital and are therefore constrained in the same ways as the hospitals' patient representatives. In still others they are volunteers, and as such, can't always be depended on to be as knowledgeable or skilled as professionals.

Insurance Company Advocates

Like hospitals, some health insurance companies are now providing patient advocates to their customers, too. Confused about treatment options? Have a question about the drug you are taking? Call your insurer's patient advocate to get answers to your questions. But don't forget – the goal of the insurance company is to be sure it doesn't spend one more penny than it has to. It's entirely possible you'll be steered toward a less expensive treatment because it's, well, less expensive. Or they might "suggest" you ask your doctor about a different drug which (surprise!) will cost them less, without regard to whether it can truly be more helpful to you.

Disease and Condition Organization Advocates

Sadly, advocates who work with some of the larger disease and condition advocacy agencies and organizations can't always be strictly focused on the patients they help. Their funding comes from large donors and pharmaceutical companies. They will be less likely to provide objective information about a treatment option than someone who is independent of those constraints will be. These organizations often provide volunteers to help, but of course, volunteerism will be limited, with no way to judge its professionalism.

As you can see, there are plenty of flavors of advocacy available to patients, but none of those listed truly serve the needs of the patient first and foremost. With their allegiance placed elsewhere, patients must question whether or not they are truly getting objective, useful assistance to improve their trek through the healthcare system.

Where Do You Fit In?

You've probably thought about becoming a patient advocate for a while... but when you contemplated the possibilities, you did so believing that you would serve the patient, and the patient alone, without all those other allegiances coming between you and the service to your patient.

That's where **private, independent, professional advocacy comes in.**

As a private, independent patient or health advocate, one who is hired by, reports to, and is paid directly by the patient to whom your allegiance is focused (or by their caregiver, employer, union or as an independent contractor to a large advocacy organization), you have the opportunity to improve the lives and healthcare experiences of hundreds or thousands of patients over the course of your career. There will be no questions about your allegiance because 100% of that allegiance is focused on improved quality and/or quantity of life for the patient you are working with. There are no outside, money-rooted barriers between you.

Patient advocacy is at the tipping point of becoming mainstream. The public has begun to recognize and embrace the need for having an independent, privately hired advocate-facilitator help them out. During the past few years we've seen patient advocacy services addressed in the New York Times, the Wall Street Journal, O Magazine, Parade Magazine, Entrepreneur Magazine, MORE Magazine, Woman's Day, Health Magazine, NPR, CNN, MSNBC and many other media outlets.

And, (this is important –underline or highlight the next sentence!) *there just aren't enough advocates to go around, nor are they located in all the places they are needed*.

For all of these reasons and more, there has never been a better time to jump in to start your own private advocacy practice. Patients need you!

How to Use This Book

I am contacted everyday by people who want to become health or patient advocates. They most often fit one of those profiles outlined in the Preface to this book, and they have a good sense that being a private patient advocate is how they can fulfill their goals. They usually have a pretty good sense of how to help someone with their healthcare system challenges, having been exposed to those challenges themselves. And they know they want to help patients directly, rather than having a hospital's rules, or an insurer's rules, or any other sort of barrier in the way to providing that assistance.

But where their hearts are strong, their prospects for employment are weak. Very few organizations exist to hire them to work directly with patients. They quickly learn that their best opinion, or perhaps their only one, is to go into business for themselves – create their own practices.

Unfortunately, the great majority of those folks are just lost when it comes to knowing how to start a business. It's not that they don't like the idea; in fact, many truly embrace the idea of being self-employed – the masters of their own domains!

But – where to start?

Start here.

That's why I wrote this book: to help those people, perhaps like you, who want to be self-employed, independent private advocates tackle the business aspects of the work. There's a big difference between explaining treatment options, and creating cash flow statements. There's a big difference, too, between helping someone lower their medical bills, and preparing to take business deductions on your own taxes. And there's a major chasm between retrieving someone's medical records, and learning to ask them to pay you for the services you've rendered.

So that's what this book will do: provide you with the business basics needed to start, then grow an independent, private advocacy practice. The easier the running-your-own business aspects are made to be, the more energy you can devote to your actual one-on-one work with your patient-clients.

Do You Have to Be Self-Employed to Be a Private, Independent Advocate?

As you can see from the descriptions in this chapter, the only way to be truly helpful to patients is to make sure there is no conflict between the work you do for them, and the goals of the organization you work for. In most cases that means that working for an employer (hospital, insurance company or even a non-profit) isn't an option because your focus will be taken away from the best interests of your patient-client.

However, the employment landscape is changing rapidly for private advocates.

An increasing number of employers are recognizing the value of providing advocates to assist their employees, especially their highest paid employees, those who cost the bottom line more when they are absent from work. Labor unions are also looking for ways to make themselves valuable to their members, and are hiring advocates as subcontractors to help them do that.

There are growing numbers of companies that are in the business of providing advocates as their service and mission. They market to individuals, not necessarily through employers or unions or other large affinity organizations. One of those companies markets to wealthy individuals only. (If you have to ask, then you can't afford them.) Others reach out to individuals like you and me, or your neighbors and friends, to offer us assistance in managing our trek through the healthcare system.

However, you should know that just like you, most of those companies are starting out. They are in desperate need of advocates who understand the basics of business-starting, marketing, and managing the bottom line; the important steps covered in this book. They aren't always hiring people outright (providing paychecks and benefits.) Instead they are working with advocates as independent contractors. (See more about working as a subcontractor in Chapter Four.) As an independent contractor, you are still considered to be self-employed.

So, even if you identify a company you would like to work for instead of starting your own practice, you should know that the business skills discussed in this book will be important for you to demonstrate when you apply for a job.

The list of private advocacy service companies updates frequently. Find a web link to the most current list of advocacy companies that may be hiring private advocates in the Resources Section in the back of this book.

From goal setting and business plan writing, to determining and pricing your services, to understanding workflow and cash flow, to getting the right licenses and insurance, to marketing and customer service, to ethics and best practices – you'll find the basics of starting your private advocacy business addressed here, and further resources for when you need more help.

This book was written for you, the person who knows he or she can do it, if only someone would give you a roadmap.

This book is your roadmap.

The Workbook

To make this even easier, I've developed a workbook to help you along the way. It's a free "extra" which you can download, and fill in (on your computer) or fill out (by hand). It contains extra advice, and extra resources, and most importantly, places for you to tailor this book to your own ideas and decisions.

Here's the link: www.HealthAdvocateResources.com/SGOP

You'll find it referenced throughout this book as you are given specific tasks to do as part of your preparation to both build a business plan and start your business.

And so, let's get started and get you into business!

Sure! Go ahead!
This is a blank page, and it's
your book, so make some notes...

Chapter One
Are You Entrepreneurial?

Starting a health advocacy practice is two things: it's advocacy and it's business. That means that any description of you, as the proprietor of an advocacy practice, must describe you as both an advocate, and as a self-employed business owner. The skills and traits needed must cover both those important aspects of what you are about to start and build.

Here are some of the qualities, situations and experiences that will lay a good foundation for building a private advocacy practice. They fall under two categories: Personality and Life Circumstances.

TASK #1

Download the Workbook that was developed to accompany this book and helps you take care of each of these steps as you learn about them. You'll find the book at:

www.HealthAdvocateResources.com/SGOP

With your Workbook in hand, you can check off, and make notes on the attributes listed in this chapter as a way to assess whether you are ready to

---

First, Let's Look at Your Entrepreneurial Personality

No – I'm not suggesting you needed to be "Most Likely to Succeed" in high school, nor did you need to be the teacher's pet. But there are definite personality traits that will be useful to you as you begin your business-starting journey. See how many of these describe you.

Refer to your Workbook, and indicate your answer to each to give you a broad idea of your likelihood for success in business (not just a patient advocacy business, but any business.)

✓ Do you thrive on challenges?

Starting and running a business is a constant source of challenges, some larger and some smaller. As a patient advocate, you'll find challenges from people who don't communicate well, people in pain, families and loved ones who have their own ideas and arguments, competitors, financial challenges, medical personnel who may not trust you and others who will put roadblocks in your way every day.

Meeting challenges is one thing. Realizing that challenges present opportunities is another. To the extent you can thrive based on your challenges, you'll find success in business.

Do you thrive on challenges?

✓ Are you a creative problem solver and decision maker?

There are two kinds of people in any workplace: those who wait around for someone to tell them what to do, and those who just get the job done, taking initiative, making decisions, trying new approaches, pulling out the stops to solve every sort of problem, and trusting their intuition that they are making good choices.

Independence is necessary in an advocacy practice because there are not many models, nor are their prescribed steps for individual patient problems. There won't be people who will tell you – or can tell you -- what to do.

Your creative problem solving and decision making chops will be tested constantly.

Are you confident and creative enough to face challenges and make decisions?

✓ Are you a risk taker?

Business owners are risk takers. Even at its best, starting and growing a new practice is a calculated risk, where "calculated" is the key word.

When you decide to go into business for yourself, you may be risking not just your money and efforts, but the security of a regular paycheck and benefits you could have had with a "real" job that you will no longer have.

Of course, you can minimize some of the risk if you start your health advocacy business part time while you continue to draw a steady paycheck, and maybe a portion of your benefits part time with that "real" job.

Further, there may also be opportunities to be an independent contractor to a larger advocacy group which allows you to focus more on advocacy and less on the business aspects of handling clients.

You may also minimize some of the risk through the planning and preparation you do before you pull the new-business trigger.

Regardless, you'll still be going out on your own, investing in your own capabilities. Are you willing to take those risks?

✓ Do you have chutzpah?

There's such a thing as being respectful of "the truth" and knowing when that truth isn't working, or isn't the right answer for your patient-client.

Medicine has long established itself as a benevolent, paternalistic bastion of people who too often put themselves on pedestals. Insurers and payer-representatives may believe that since they control the purse strings, they have a right to say "yes" or "no" to recommendations. When either of those well-established institutions plays God with your client, it may not be in his or her best interests.

Sometimes, as an effective health advocate, you'll need to be willing to buck the establishment, to ask questions that make "the Gods" unhappy, and to insist some professionals do things they don't want to do.

Are you capable of sticking up for your client even when the tide turns against you?

✓ Are you a people person?

Patient advocacy isn't really about medicine or science or insurance or billing. It's about people who have problems with those aspects of their healthcare. Genuinely liking people – even people who may be upset, frustrated, cranky, angry, sick or hurt, or any other emotion – and being able to work with them under those circumstances, is paramount. If you don't like to work with people, you won't like being a health advocate.

Included in this attribute is the ability to be empathic but not to let that empathy get in your way.

Do you get along with people when they are at their best, and their worst? Can you balance empathy with business to serve your clients well?

✓ Are you a good listener?

One of the most important people skills you'll need is the ability to listen. When a patient or caregiver hires you, they aren't hiring you to hear YOUR stories, or YOUR experiences.

They are hiring you to listen to them. Active listening, which sometimes includes the ability to "hear between the lines" is one of the most important skills you need to bring to your advocacy work.

Are you a good listener?

✓ Are you self-disciplined?

Working for yourself may seem like utopia. Being your own boss means you get to make money through all your own choices and decisions, and take time off when you want to, right?

Not exactly.

Working for yourself requires a great deal of discipline, especially if you choose to work from home. It requires a commitment that will override the temptation created by anything else. From arguing kids, to the barking dog, to the neighbor mowing her lawn, to the weeds in your garden, to your laundry, those soap operas and talk shows – you need to tune them out and stay focused.

Further, it's a myth that you'll be your own boss. Each person you work for at any given moment, plus all those you hope will hire you – they are all your bosses. In fact, you may have dozens of bosses at a time.

Self-discipline is an essential trait for anyone who is self-employed, including health advocates.

Can you focus on your work and shut out the other tasks and fun that may be calling your name?

✓ Are you trustworthy?

The two most important aspects of any individual's life are his health and his money. A potential client will hire you when they believe they can trust you with those two most important things.

You won't have to hand over your credit report, or get your high school teacher to vouch for you, but you'll need both a trustworthy approach and an honorable reputation as you begin laying your groundwork with potential clients.

Do others trust you? Should they?

✓ Are you a patient person?

No pun intended here, but patience is a necessary trait for both the business and advocacy corners of your business. Clients won't come knocking at your door the moment you hang out your shingle, nor will you be profitable overnight.

But there's also a point where being too patient won't help you either. You need to be IMpatient enough to know when it's time to go to collections because a client hasn't paid you, or to recommend to a client that she change doctors because you know she's not getting the attention she deserves.

Is your patience level evenly balanced to accommodate for the people and situations you'll be juggling?

Do You Need to Be a Nurse or Have Clinical Experience to Be an Effective Patient or Health Advocate?

In the early days of private, professional advocacy, a sizeable controversy arose over the question of whether or not someone needed to have a nursing or other clinical background to be an effective patient advocate. In fact, at one of the early advocacy conferences, some attendees who had no clinical background were shunned by those who did!

It's a fair question: Do you need clinical expertise to be a good health advocate?

The simple answer is NO, you do not have to have a clinical background, nor will not having a clinical background inhibit your ability to be highly respected or successful in the profession of private advocacy.

First, there are many forms of advocacy that are not necessarily medical care related. Billing and claims advocates, for example, need knowledge of the system, but not of medicine itself. Patient safety advocates focus on procedures and not on medicine. Case management, research, mediation, home health care – these are all advocacy services that may not require clinical knowledge.

Further, some services might not be as effectively performed by someone who spent a career working "inside" the system. Sometimes it requires someone who doesn't have that history to ask the right questions to get their patient-clients what they need. Some clinical providers are so ingrained in the system that they don't know how to ask questions an advocate needs to ask. (We'll discuss this more thoroughly in Chapter Twelve).

Some of the longest-in-business, most well-known and respected private health advocates started their practices having had no clinical background. Ken Schueler (for whom the Schueler Patient Advocacy Compass Award was named), Elisabeth Russell, and Joanna Smith who founded NAHAC, all highly respected, long time private patient advocates; none of them had clinical backgrounds when they started their practices. What they did have in common were stories that compelled them in the direction of advocacy. A passion for the work was their foundation.

All that said, private advocacy is a perfect next step for nurses and others, including a growing number of medical doctors (MDs and DOs) who are establishing private advocacy practices. It allows them the chance to refocus on the very reasons they chose healthcare as a career to begin with – the needs, wishes and best interests of their clients.

✓ Can you be flexible?

I decided long ago that flexibility is the key to a long and happy life. That's true in business, too.

Flexibility may mean that if a client calls you because she's been hospitalized at 7 PM, you're willing to put your *we've-had-reservations-for-a-month* dinner plans on hold to attend to her.

Flexibility may mean that if your bank won't loan you money until September, you're willing to ask Great Uncle Marvin for a bridge loan until then.

The definition of flexibility is that you never know when you'll need it. You just need to be "it" when the time comes.

No one is suggesting you need to wrap your arms behind your back so you look like a pretzel, or to be a Cirque de Soleil performer. But do you have the flexibility to handle surprises on a constant basis?

✓ Do you understand your weaknesses?

Having a good sense of what you are good at vs what you aren't (or even what you don't like to do) provides you with two good pieces of information:

First, it gives you some sense of gaps that need to be filled. For example, I really don't like bookkeeping. I do OK with it except that I resent the time I have to spend doing it. It's a gap I look to fill.

Second, understanding your weaknesses helps you define what you may still need to learn. Maybe if someone taught me a simple way to do my bookkeeping, I wouldn't resent it so much.

Typical business weaknesses include not understanding financial information (cash flow, budgeting, price setting, etc) or not understanding marketing (advertising, public relations, websites, etc). Additional weaknesses that relate to patient advocacy will a lack of understanding how the healthcare system works, or being afraid to speak up to authority figures.

We'll address a number of these typical weak spots throughout this book, but knowing what they are will help you better understand how much effort you need to put in to filling those gaps.

Are you willing to constantly assess your weaknesses and then take steps to overcome them?

✓ **Are you willing to expect and accept payment?**

One of the biggest differences between people who succeed in business vs those who do not, is the mindset of "My expertise is worth paying for."

So many advocates have big hearts and just want to be helpful. Someone who needs help approaches them, and they simply give away their expertise. Period.

While volunteerism is a noble cause, it doesn't work in business. "Just helping" won't keep a business afloat. Giving away your services for any reason, whether it's because you are nervous about asking for money, or because you aren't sure your capabilities are worth the money someone would pay you, the effect is the same. You'll go out of business. You may succeed as someone who has assisted people who need help, but you will have failed as a business owner.

We'll be looking at how to talk about money with your clients later in this book. It will be important that you learn to ask for what you deserve. Making that leap from "I can do this" to "I am worthy of being paid for this" isn't easy, but it's vitally necessary if you expect to build a thriving practice.

Are you willing to ask for the money that is owed you?

✓ **Do you learn well from mistakes?**

"Once burned, twice shy." I'm always surprised at how many people think they subscribe to that belief, but continue doing the same things that got them in trouble the first, second or third times they tried them.

An example: a patient calls asking for information about your patient advocacy services. Within the call, they tell you what they need help with, and you help them – right then and there. Now they no longer need your services because you've already helped them solve the problem. You hang up the phone and sigh. So much for that client, who now won't need to hire you because you gave away the farm.

Do you view that as an imperative that you figure out a new way of dealing with potential clients on the phone? Do you reach out to others asking them to help you get past that mistake? Or do you do the same thing the next time?

Insanity is defined as repeating the same behavior and expecting different results. Can you avoid insanity?

✓ **Do you have a thick skin?**

No doubt you've heard the truism that you can't please everyone all the time, and there is no place that's truer than in business. Further, for all the reasons cited in this chapter –

when people are sick, and cranky, and their very life and financial stability are being threatened, they are bound to be times that they won't be happy. And "when your client ain't happy – ain't nobody happy."

You need the ability to realize that in most cases, their dissatisfaction isn't personal – it's how they are coping. Since you represent all the steps and emotions that they must cope with, you may be the target of their discontent more often than you can imagine.

It may take a while to develop those emotional calluses, and even better, develop that balance between being calloused and being empathetic. But a true professional knows how to balance those two successfully for both her benefit and her client's.

How thick is your skin?

Now Let's Look at Your Life Circumstances

In addition to personality traits, your life circumstances and experiences will either help you build a practice, or will get in the way. See where you stand with any of the following:

✓ Do you have money in the bank?

No doubt you've heard of people starting a business on a shoe-string budget. They do exist - but they are rare. More common – too common – are those who don't have enough money put away to give themselves the freedom to start their businesses and grow them at a good pace.

Some texts will suggest you have six months' worth of bill-paying capabilities put away to drawn on when you need to. Others will suggest you win the lottery. Still others will tell you to "borrow" from your retirement.

I don't suggest any of those. I suggest you take the important financial planning steps that will tell you how much you'll need. We'll tackle those steps in Chapter Seven.

✓ Are you healthy?

Starting, growing and maintaining a business is not for the faint of heart! And it's not for someone who isn't a basically healthy individual.

Count on stress, long hours, and a maximized learning curve which requires monumental attention and energy, especially in the early years. You will also need to be available to your clients, sometimes 24/7/365, and if you are dealing with illness yourself, that may not be possible.

There is one exception to this need to be healthy. Some advocates come to their work because they deal with a specific disease or condition, and that's what makes them the perfect person to work with someone else who faces the same diagnosis. Specifically I know of an advocate who has MS, and another who has lupus. In both cases they work only with clients who have those same diagnoses. You can imagine how empathetic and understanding they must be with those clients.

✓ Do you have a support system in place?

According to the Small Business Administration, it will probably take you three to five years for your business to sustain itself, and for it to be considered "profitable."

That's a lot of pressure. You'll need a support system to help you out with money, time and understanding.

Money – to keep your bills paid. A support system, either in the way of a partner or spouse who can keep the mortgage covered and the lights on (not to mention gas in your tank) will keep you out of trouble with your creditors.

Time – because your 12 and 14 hour days won't allow time for much else as you build your business. Gone are the days of eight-hours-working-for-THE-MAN. As a business owner you'll put in those eight hours and more, and that's before you tackle your bookkeeping, invest some energy in your marketing, and meet with your lawyer to be sure your business forms are up-to-date and legal. If your support system (usually your family) isn't willing to allow that time, then it will take far longer to build your business than those three to five years – if you can do it at all.

Understanding – goes along with time. If your spouse or partner isn't understanding about his or her need to support the time and money needs you'll have, if you have to argue every time a dime needs spending, then your energy will be focused on that argument and not on building your business. If your children demand time that you don't have to give, then their resentment will pray on your mind and make you feel guilty.

Be sure your support system understands what will be involved before you take the leap to self-employment.

✓ Do you have a good network in place?

It's highly likely that the first people to hire you will come from the people you already know – your network.

Family, friends, neighbors, former work colleagues, people from your church or synagogue – these are all people who know you well enough already to trust you, and to trust you can help them.

In some cases they won't pay you with money as you get started. You might work with them to gain experience and a track record.

Over time, word of mouth will help you build a network. But having a strong network in place to begin with can help you launch your new health advocacy business much more quickly than if you don't know many people.

✓ **Do you have advocacy experience?**

If you don't have some basic advocacy skills to begin with, you will not succeed as a health or patient advocate right away. The learning curve is steep, and it's not something you can learn from a YouTube video or reading a book or group of articles.

To be clear, I'm not talking about running an advocacy business (legal entities, marketing, financial statements, etc) – that's what this book is for.

What I am talking about is a basic understanding of how to advocate for another human being; navigating the healthcare system, or reducing a medical bill – performing the actual advocacy skills themselves.

Would you drive a taxi in Beijing tomorrow? Why not? Most likely because you don't know your way around, and you wouldn't understand the language.

Same with health advocacy. Knowing your way around the healthcare system, and understanding the language are both important keys to success. No, you do not need to be a nurse or have other clinical experience, but knowing what the right resources are, and understanding where your client's problem fits into the bigger picture will be the keys to helping the people who pay you to help them.

So, Now, What Do You Think?

After all that, do you still want to start a private, independent health advocacy practice?

I hope so!

Whether you've come away from this chapter believing you're the perfect candidate, or you now have a list of attributes to work on, or a nagging suspicion that you should be thinking twice...

Whatever you do – keep reading.

Chapter Two
What Skills Are Needed to Run a Successful Practice?

Before I wrote my first book, I received some sage advice from my agent. She told me, "The worst book ever written will be a resounding success if it has great marketing. The best book ever written will never be seen by reader #1 if the author doesn't understand the business side of being an author."

Because I have spent 25+ years of my life either working with small businesses to help them succeed, or attending to my own businesses as I started them and grew them, I understood perfectly what she was saying. It didn't matter how engaging, useful or well-written my book was. If I didn't know how to handle the business and marketing sides of writing a successful book, then my efforts were doomed.

Through the process, I also realized there were other skills I needed to have. I needed to be able to organize my thoughts in ways I had never done before. I needed to be able to type fast enough to keep up with my thought process. I needed to be able to spell (spellcheckers tend to cause trouble) and punctuate correctly. I had no knowledge of medicine, yet I was writing a book about healthcare, so I needed to seek advice from others who could be helpful – not just the agent who had already provided some good input, but from doctors, insurance people, other patients, librarians and even editors who would help me make my book more readable.

Further, I needed to do things I really dislike doing. Math – in the form of budgeting, cash flow and tracking expenses, plus obtaining ISBN numbers, learning how to list the book at Amazon and other book-selling sites, setting up book signings when I had speaking opportunities, and many more.

I even had to learn how to handle very unpleasant tasks like telling the graphic designer that I really did NOT like his design for my book cover (I ended up designing my own), to working with lawyers on contracts with the publisher (which taught me that those contracts are set up so that everyone else makes money – except me, the author.) And, one of the most difficult lessons for anyone who goes into business, is learning how to separate business from personal. If someone says no, or decides not to hire you, or objects to your pricing, or gets upset with you – it's not personal. It's business. But – still – ouch. (See Chapter One about developing a tough skin.)

So for my first book[1], I listened, learned, and diligently developed, then followed my business and marketing plans. I learned in a big way that my advisors were right. It was not about writing a book – it was about business, and mostly marketing. I've been able to use that sage advice through my second book, and now this, my third one, too.

You will find the same to be true for starting and building a health advocacy practice.

No matter what job you have, or what business you want to start, there is a set of skills that are necessary to get it done, and get it done well. While those core skills will address whatever your product or service, is, the supporting business needs and services will be just as important, and sometimes even more important to your success.

Chances are, you already have these skills – but you may not yet realize it. Perhaps you've worked at a job that provided some background. For example, if you were a nurse, you'll probably understand the basics about how the healthcare system functions. If you worked in coding and billing, then you have a head start on the skills needed to offer medical claims and billing reviews for clients. If you worked in a small private practice, then you understand more about actually running a business than others do.

Or maybe you've volunteered through a local advocacy group, through your church or synagogue, or even as the cookie mom for the Girl Scouts. Even though you probably won't sell cookies through your advocacy practice, you can definitely learn about organizing other people, being resourceful, answering questions and certainly – patience.

The good news is that you don't have to have all these skills yourself.

Unlike the personality traits and demeanors we reviewed in Chapter One, the skill areas we'll list here don't necessarily require you be the only skilled person who performs them.

In fact, rarely can one person do everything by him or herself – at least not as well as it could be done with help. Even if you are a one-person business or an independent contractor, there will be times you should ask someone else to help you.

For example, I have no employees, but I do have freelancers (also called subcontractors) who help me with web development, editing and financial work (especially taxes.) Those folks are much better than I am at those tasks. No sense butting my head against a wall trying to do them myself.

Further, even for the skills you are good at, there are times it will be better to call in help, because the time it takes to perform them will actually cost you time that you could spend earning income. A good example: in the time it would take me to fight my way through Turbo-Tax each year, I can make $1,000 in consulting fees. So why would I spend so many

---

1   *You Bet Your Life! The 10 Mistakes Every Patient Makes (How to Fix Them to Get the Healthcare You Deserve)* was my first book, written for patients, which is now used as part of the curriculum for several patient advocacy programs in the United States.

miserable hours doing my taxes when my CPA charges me a total of $350? It's not just that she is better at figuring my taxes than I am. She saves me time I can put to better use.

So let's look at the skills that you may need, or need access to, as you start your advocacy business. Which ones do you have covered? Which ones do you still need to learn more about? Which ones can you hire help for? Which ones don't apply to your business?

TASK #2

Many of the skills you might need to start and grow your business are listed both here in your book, and in the Health Advocate Practice Workbook, too. Go through the lists checking off the right column for each: the ones you can do and want to do, the ones you can do but could delegate, and the ones you can't do and will need to delegate.

....

A reminder that you can download the free companion workbook at www.HealthAdvocateResources.com/SGOP

Advocacy Skills:

- ◆ Knowledge of how the healthcare system works
- ◆ Knowledge of how patients and caregivers think
- ◆ Knowledge of how doctors' offices and hospitals function
- ◆ Navigation
- ◆ Knowledge of HIPAA or Canadian privacy regulations
- ◆ Shared decision making
- ◆ Billing and claims systems
- ◆ Flexibility[2]
- ◆ Creative problem solving
- ◆ Research skills – for learning about diagnoses or treatment options, finding good professionals to work with and more
- ◆ Others (list the ones you know you will need for the services you hope to offer – more in Chapter Four.)

---

2   Flexibility is the one attribute needed in every aspect of business.
    (Flexibility is the key to a long and happy life!)

People Skills:

- Empathy
- Good telephone manners
- Strong handshake
- Ability to put yourself in someone else's shoes, to see things from other points of view
- Ability to manage expectations – explain what can be expected, both the good and the bad
- Ability to address unpleasant topics in a professional manner
- Facilitation, often communications between professionals and your clients
- Negotiation/bargaining/mediation skills for working with clients and their loved ones, or encouraging medical personal to see things your way
- Flexibility[2]
- Networking with other like-minded individuals (and maybe a few who think very differently

Business Skills[3]

- Professionalism
- Flexibility[2]
- Financial projections, budgeting, money management, tax filing, and cash flow
- Basic bookkeeping (especially understanding tax deductions, tracking expenses)
- Technology management (using a computer, using a smartphone, managing email, creating spreadsheets, word processing, webcasts, teleconferences, others)
- Record keeping, time tracking
- Time management
- Understanding insurance
- Understanding use of, and need for, business contracts, their clauses and provisions

---

3 Business skills are what this book is about so don't fret over these – read this book!

Marketing Skills[4]

- ◆ Understanding target audiences
- ◆ Knowing how to reach target audiences
- ◆ Choosing the right marketing tactics
- ◆ Creativity
- ◆ Networking / elbow rubbing
- ◆ Social media
- ◆ Public speaking
- ◆ Assessment of efforts (return on money spent)

These lists are just a start. Chances are that you are very good at some of these things, passably good at others, and for still others, you have no idea how to even ask the questions.

According to the US Small Business Administration (SBA), the reason most small businesses fail isn't because they don't know how to provide or deliver whatever their core business is (in your case, your core business will be helping patients and caregivers improve their experience with the healthcare system). Instead, they fail because they haven't learned to manage the business aspects of their work. Uncle Gino may make great pizza, but if he doesn't know how to keep his books, and spends all his cash in June, not saving enough to pay July's rent – well then – Uncle Gino will go out of the pizza business.

The reason you purchased this book was to help you better understand those business-knowledge requirements you'll need to address. So don't fret if that list of skills looks overwhelming, or if you checked off "need help" for most. That's why we're in this together.

In Chapter Five we'll be developing a "gap list;" that is, a list of things you either need help with, or need to learn in order to fill the gaps.

But we have one more step before we develop our gap list. We're going to begin describing your core business – the reasons you chose health advocacy to begin with.

---

4   For do-it-your-selfers, see *The Health Advocate's Marketing Handbook* - discounts available in the Resources section in the back of this book

Sure! Go ahead!
This is a blank page, and it's
your book, so make some notes...

Chapter Three
Where Are You Going?
Let's Look at Plans and Goals

We've made some interesting assessments during the past two chapters. You should now have a good idea of whether you have the personality and demeanor for being in business for yourself, a list of skills you will need to bring to the business table to succeed, and an assessment of whether you have the chops to make it happen.

In the minds of most business advisors, that means it's time to begin building your business plan! Oh yes – those words every beginner entrepreneur dreads – "THE BUSINESS PLAN" !

What I've never been able to understand is how anyone thinks that a newbie to the starting -a-business world can possibly know how to build a business plan. How can you prepare something useful when you don't understand what most of it means?

Which is why I wrote this book for you. And why I like to do things backwards.

Instead of beginning with a business plan, we're going to begin with basics – those basics that will support your planning. Later, in Chapter Fourteen, we'll put your business plan together.

"No" to Your Business Plan – but "Yes" to Your Goals

While we may not try to commit your future business to a formal business plan yet, we do want to take a look at your goals. Everything from your personal goals to your business goals, and the places they may intersect.

What we hope to accomplish here is some very top level, beginning goal setting. At this point, determining your goals will be preliminary; you don't have a lot of information to base them on yet. Perhaps, for now, they are better described as your educated hopes or wishes.

The answers aren't right or wrong – they are right for you. They may even change over time. Answering them will help you determine how to move forward, and whether or not you're ready to strike out on your own as a health advocate in private practice.

Note: You may not know the answers to all these questions yet. That's kind of the point.

We're going through this exercise now to give you a basic direction, and to help you understand what you are about to learn in the rest of this book. Sometimes the best way to learn is to understand the questions that need answering.

That means we'll revisit your goals later in the book, too. You'll be able to adjust your answers based on what you've learned, and what your capabilities and possibilities are.

TASK #3

Your answers to each of the following questions will be
important to your success.

There are no right or wrong answers – they will be individual to you,
and whatever you want them to be.

We'll morph these questions, and your answers,
into your business plan in Chapter Fourteen.

You'll find these questions in your Workbook,
just waiting for you to take a stab at the answers.

Personal Goals:

Answer questions like:

- What is your story? Why do you want to help others journey through their healthcare experience?

- Why do you want to start your own business?

- What personal goals do you hope to satisfy?

- Are you starting because you want to achieve something? Or because you want to leave something else behind? (If it's because you want to leave something else behind, how will being in business for yourself help you accomplish that?)

- Is this a long term career plan? Or something to keep you busy in retirement?

- What sort of licensing or credentialing will you seek?
- What support do you have from those around you?
- Are you trying to prove something to yourself? Or prove something to others?

Service Goals:

- What advocacy services do you plan to offer?
- Will you start with a shorter list of services, then expand? Or will you focus on one or two types of services and not try to grow beyond those?
- How many clients can you handle in a week, a month or a year?
- What will your availability be? Monday through Friday from 8 to 5? Evenings? Weekends? Holidays? 24/7? Remember – being flexible is one of those important attributes for success.
- What will your geography be? Will you work only with local clients? Or will you expand farther (state or province, national, international?)
- What will you do if someone asks you to help them in some way you aren't prepared to help them?
- What will you do if someone is too difficult to work with?
- What will you do if a client dies?
- Will you perform all your services for profit? Or will you do some pro bono work? (free, donated time)

What Should You Call Yourself?

Since today's health advocates are pioneers, establishing a profession that didn't really exist even five years ago, at least in today's form, it has been a struggle coming up with a name that would be recognizable to enough people, and not get mixed up with other professions.

Some people have told me they object to the term "advocate" because they think it suggests a contentious relationship (as it does in the law), as if the client needs protection from the big-bad-provider, rather than someone who will facilitate the relationship.

Navigator seems like a good term, except that many advocates don't navigate – they negotiate or mediate or do math (billing advocates!) Further, the term "navigator" has been co-opted by the cancer community, and now many navigators are found working in hospitals with cancer patients. Private, independent advocates and navigators don't want to be confused with those who are paid by hospitals.

No recommendations here, but instead a list of possibilities, some of which you might want to adopt for the name of your company, or to use as keywords for your online presence.

- concierge
- patient advocate
- health advocate
- navigator
- health advisor
- service coordinator or facilitator
- care planner
- care manager
- nurse advocate
- ombudsman
- claims reviewer

Credentials Goals:

- What courses or programs do you intend to take or participate in to expand your skill set, or improve your ability to grow your business?
- Are you licensed? Do you need to be?
- Will you join advocacy organizations? If so, which ones?
- How do you plan to network with other advocates?

Income Goals:

- How much profit do you hope to make: In your first year?
- In your second year?
- In your third year?
- How will you handle a situation where a client refuses to pay you?

Future Goals:

- How will you grow your business? Since you can't expand the number of hours in a day, will you hire new people? Or subcontractors? Or increase your fees or list of services?
- What will you do when it comes time to retire? Sell your business? Close your business?

Should You Tell Others You're Planning to Open Your Own Practice?

I would.

I'm asked this question frequently by those who are in the early decision-making stages of whether or not they want to start their own practices. They know in their hearts what they want to do. But their heads are telling them to be cautious.

I can't think of anyone I have ever met who was successful as a result of being cautious. Not one.

So by all means – start tooting your horn. Begin telling people that you're exploring the possibility of becoming an independent health advocate – and follow that statement with a question, "If you had a health challenge, would you hire me?" Or "If you had trouble organizing your medical bills, would you hire me?" In addition to the benefit of this ad hoc market research, it will put your friends and acquaintances on notice that you're giving this serious consideration.

The minute they need someone's help, you'll come to mind. It's like a running start on your marketing.

Once again I say, *"What I've never been able to understand is how anyone thinks that a newbie to the starting-a-business world can ever understand how to build a business plan. How can you prepare something useful when you don't understand what most of it means?"*

Now you have a far better idea of the depth of understanding you need as you kick off your new business.

So let's hunker down and figure out what you need to know to answer all these questions.

Chapter Four
Your Core Business:
What Services Will You Offer?

Most "start-your-own (<u>fill-in-the-blank)</u> business" books which focus on service businesses contain a chapter that outlines the many services that can be offered within that discipline. For example, a start-your-own-math-tutoring business book would suggest a list of services like algebra tutoring, geometry tutoring, tutoring GED students, helping with word problems (remember those?) or even preparing for the math section of the SAT or ACT test.

Math tutoring has been around since the first kid was failing math, and that kid's father couldn't remember how to bisect a parallelogram. As a result, any parent who has ever had a child who couldn't cut the math mustard knows to go looking for a math tutor, and knows what kinds of help to ask about. There is no mystery to math tutoring services.

But there's plenty of mystery to health and patient advocacy. As a profession and as a private practice, patient advocacy is so new that few advocates have a clear sense of what services to offer, and few potential clients know what kinds of services to expect, or even to ask about. In many parts of the United States and Canada, clients don't even know that someone might be available to help them, much less know how to describe or name the services they will need.

For those of us with an entrepreneurial spirit – that's good news! We love to be the trailblazers, the ones who begin to set the standards, and to boldly go where no health advocates have gone before. We're pleased to list possible services, and decide what to call them, and help to market them and educate the public, our potential clients.

(And sure – for those of you who are a little less entrepreneurial, but still ready to be early aficionados of this new profession – we're happy to bring you along for the ride.)

The master list of possible services currently being offered by health and patient advocates can be found online at the AdvoConnection website.[5] (We'll look closer at AdvoConnection later in this book.)

Those services are broken into categories, and are listed here (and updated on occasion, so this may not be the latest list.[6]) They are:

- ♦ Medical / Navigational Assistance
- ♦ Background Research: Diagnosis, Treatment Options and more
- ♦ Hospital Bedside, or Travel / Accompaniment to Appointments
- ♦ Shared Decision Making
- ♦ Pain Management
- ♦ Geriatric / Eldercare or Home Health Services
- ♦ Mediation (Helping families manage health-related disagreements)
- ♦ Mental Health and Substance Abuse Assistance
- ♦ Medical Bill Reviewing / Health Insurance / Payer Assistance
- ♦ Pregnancy, Birth and Pediatric Assistance
- ♦ Integrative, Holistic, Complementary and Alternative Therapies
- ♦ Prevention (Prescription Drug Review, Health/Wellness Coaching, Weight Loss, Immunity, Others)
- ♦ Medical Tourism Coordination
- ♦ Legal Assistance including SSDI (Medical / Healthcare Related)
- ♦ Other (specify)

As you look at these categories, you probably have a good sense of which ones you cover with your skills, and which ones you don't. You may also be thinking that it will be easy to define which services you can offer, and which ones you can't.

But if you make those assessments based simply on your own skills, you will not only be shooting yourself in your new business foot, but you may be setting yourself up for failure.

Why? Because you are not the person who defines the services you offer.... Your clients will be the ones who form your list of services.

Let's look at that statement more closely by offering an example.

Mrs. Jehosephat calls you because her husband has become an invalid, she can no longer take care of him, her children are fighting over what to do with him in order to help her, and she just can't cope.

You listen carefully to Mrs. J – and realize that you don't really know what to do to help her, or that you have an idea of what it takes, but you just don't have those skills.

---

6   Each of these categories is also broken into subcategories.   The most up-to-date list of categories and subcategories of services can be found at: www.AdvoConnection.com/services.htm

What do you do next?

1. Tell Mrs. J you are so very sorry her life has taken such a difficult turn. Then tell her you're not the person who can help her.
2. Tell Mrs. J you are so very sorry her life has taken such a difficult turn. Then apologize, and tell her you can't help her, but you'll find someone who can help. Then contact a fellow advocate who offers the necessary services and connect the two of them.
3. Tell Mrs. J you are so very sorry her life has taken such a difficult turn, and that you would be glad to discuss further the services you offer that might help her. Then go find a course you can take to ramp up and learn how to help her.
4. Tell Mrs. J you are so very sorry her life has taken such a difficult turn, and that you would be glad to discuss further the services you offer that might help her. Then find a fellow advocate who will help Mrs. J while working as a subcontractor to you.

What Do We Call the People We Work With?

Throughout this book I refer to the people we perform advocacy services for as patients, sometimes customers, and most often, clients or patient-clients.

I used to always call them patients, until one day it was pointed out that "patient" is very much a medical term, and that we are making a concerted effort to help the people we do work for understand that we will not, that we cannot, perform medical services for them. Therefore it made sense to move away from the concept of doing work for "patients" – as a good way to manage everyone's expectations about the relationship.

The word "customer' doesn't seem to work well. Most of the time we think of customers as people who walk into a store and buy a product. Very retail sounding. There's no relationship or expertise implied, both attributes that advocates offer.

Other professions, such as lawyers, or accountants, agents, or even many hairdressers call the people they work with "clients." The word "client" implies an ongoing relationship that offers a service and level of expertise.

So – the person we actually work for, the person who compensates us for our work, is the client. But we do need to make one distinction, and that is, that sometimes the client is not the person we perform services for. The person we actually help might be an adult child of an elderly "patient" or even the employer of the person who needs help.

In this book, I've tried to make the distinction by referring to clients, and to patient-clients (the person you're helping.) But in truth, the jury is out on how to make that distinction.

Of most importance is just to be sure that everyone knows exactly who you are referring to, no matter what you call them, or to whom. Communication is about clarity, no matter what words you use to describe the people you work with.

If you answered #1, which in effect simply sends Mrs. Johesephat elsewhere, then you might as well give this book away to someone else, and forget about being in business for yourself. Sending a potential client away, unless they have asked for something that is illegal, or not in the realm of possibility (or advocacy services), or unless they want your services for free is never a good answer. (See a discussion on volunteerism in Chapter Eight)

If you answered #2, you have a better chance of business success. At least you know not to simply dismiss a potential client who really needs help. And sometimes finding someone else to help, and bowing out of the relationship can be the right answer.

Answers #3 and #4 are the best for growing your business as an advocate. In the short term, you might choose #4, simply because Mrs. J needs help now and you aren't ready now. Choice #3 will mean that you recognize that's a service you, too, could offer if you knew how, even though, for business growth. Maybe it's time to find a course that can teach you how to handle it.

Specialty Services and Niches

Most new advocates choose to generalize; that is, they offer navigational type services, or general claims and billing services, or they focus on the broad picture of geriatric care.

But some advocates are finding success by being a little more 'niche'. Instead of a broad list of services, they choose one or two and become the known experts in those areas. Some accomplish this by subcontracting; that is, make themselves available to be hired by other advocates for their niche expertise. Others broaden their geography or offer their services online, which means they have a larger pool of potential clients.

Examples: One nurse practitioner offers advocacy services focusing on pain management only. She doesn't offer medical services, so she is not writing prescriptions or orders for therapy. What she is doing is helping clients manage their pain by helping them collaborate with their doctors, teaching them some biofeedback methods for pain control, and staying up on the latest in research to help advise both her clients and their doctors about new methods, drugs or other treatments that may be helpful. She is paid by clients, but her clients' doctors have learned that their relationships with their pain patients have improved, so they refer patients to her, too.

Another example is an advocate whose sole practice focuses on family mediation, recognizing that so many family arguments stem from medical and health challenges. There are adult children all over the country, just like Mrs. Jehosephat's, who are trying to figure out what to do about Mom and Dad. Should they sell the family homestead to pay for the nursing home? Should dad be kept on life support? How can they spark a discussion about advance directives?

If you are interested in offering a niche service as opposed to establishing a more general practice, then there are two ways you can do so. You can start out in a general practice, but focus your marketing just on the types of clients/services you hope to attract. Or you can start out only in your niche and never waver from it.

The key to the right approach is some market research to learn whether or not there are enough people in your geographic area (whether it's local, regional or international) who will need your services, and have the means to hire you. Market research is its own discipline, a book by itself, and we have not addressed it here, although we will touch on it in Chapter Nine (Marketing). [7]

Subcontracting Advocacy Services

Subcontracting services is a two-sided relationship that helps two or more advocates team together to provide services to a client. You, as a professional advocate, might find yourself on either side of the subcontracting relationship.

(Let's be clear on terminology here. The terms 'independent contractor', 'contractor,' 'subcontractor' or 'freelancer' are used interchangeably for these kinds of business relationships.)

One advocate takes the lead. That's usually the person who is hired by the client, but doesn't have either the skills, or perhaps the time, to provide the services needed. The lead advocate then finds someone else (we'll call him an assisting advocate) who does have the skills and the time. The two of them agree to work together, signing a contract that describes how the assisting advocate will provide the necessary services to the client, and in consideration of that work, the lead advocate will pay the assisting advocate a portion of the money paid by the client.

An example: In Mrs. Jehosephat's case (see page 42) The lead advocate would find a family mediator who would help Mrs. J and her children figure out what approach would work best for all involved. Mrs. J would pay the lead advocate, say $1000 for the services, and because the assisting advocate performed all the advocacy services, the lead advocate would pay the assisting $900 and keep $100 of the transaction. After all, the lead was the person who got the original phone call, and the lead was the one who had to do all the administrative work. But the assisting advocate was the one who did the advocacy work.

Subcontracting can be win-win-win. The client gets what she needs, the lead advocate knows her marketing worked, and that people need this service, and the assisting advocate was paid for supplying the actual advocacy services.

As a private advocate, you might find yourself the lead advocate one day, and the assisting advocate another day. Some larger private advocacy practices work entirely with subcontractors; the principle owners do no direct client advocacy work themselves.

There are some legal considerations to working this way, including subcontractor agreements and insurance. Agreements and contracts will be addressed in Chapter Ten.

---

7 Find market research links in the Resources section at the back of this book.

Projecting Your Service offerings

Despite the fact that your target audiences (your clients or customers) will be the ones defining your eventual service offerings. It's still important to begin with a list of services you hope to offer, and to have a good sense of who will perform them.

It's time to pull out your Workbook again and make that list.

TASK #4

This task, then will determine what services your practice will offer, realizing that they will eventually be massaged by the requests potential clients will make. But you need to begin with a core service offering, so it's time to quantify what that core will be.

Some starter questions are offered in your Workbook, so give it a try.

Now that you've worked through the master lists of services and determined which ones your practice will focus on, I'll remind you about flexibility.

"Flexibility" shows up on the skills lists frequently (Chapter Two) and that flexibility may never be more important than it is with your services list. If you determine that all you want to do is treatment research, but people keep asking you if you can help them make up lists of questions to take to the doctor – listen, and adjust, or go out of business.

Next up: Is it time for you to go back to school?

Chapter Five

Mind the Gap!
(Do You Need To Go Back To School?)

Having covered the skills you need, and the services you want to begin offering, you may be getting the sense that there's... just... something... well....

You aren't sure you're ready. It has seemed like such a great idea to become an independent professional advocate, but, now you can't be sure because there seems to be such a gap, maybe a real chasm in what you need to know!

If that's how you feel, then know that you are not alone! Few people (if any) feel like they know everything they need to know to get started.

So if you are concerned that there are holes in your knowledge bank, then you are probably right. It's time for us to figure out where those holes are, and then, how to fill them.

Your Knowledge Gap Analysis

Now that you've taken a good look at the skills you'll need to start and grow a private advocacy practice, and you've listed the services you would like to offer in the short and longer terms, it should be fairly simple to see what gaps exist in your knowledge.

TASK #5

It's time to determine your knowledge gaps.

Go through the many lists you have made: your skill sets, and the services you hope to offer, then circle or highlight the ones you know will require further study. If you want to, you can rank them, too, based on how much further study they will require. For example, you might give those things that would only require a bit of brushing up a 1, but those things you know nothing about a 5 - or anything in between.

Don't worry about doing the analysis part just yet.
For now we are just determining where those gaps are.

All set? OK. Let's review your findings:

If you are a nurse or have enjoyed another health-related career until now, then your gaps are probably mostly centered on the business aspects of getting started.

If you do not have a clinical background, then your gaps may be evenly divided between the medical / navigational side of the work, and the business side – or – maybe your interests lean toward the medical billing and claims type work, or perhaps your gaps are across the board.

You may find additional gaps in the knowledge needed to work with a senior or elderly population. Or maybe your challenges will be about using technology, or learning how to develop a cash flow statement....

Your assessment of these gaps is your gap analysis. You should be able to come away with a good sense of what knowledge you still need to acquire before starting your business.

Filling Those Gaps

Once you know what's missing, you'll need to find a way to fill those holes. Here are some ideas for do-it-yourselfers:

1. Learn the skill or knowledge bank yourself. You can take courses, or attend classes[8], or contact someone who can tutor or mentor you. Look for these kinds of programs online, or phone your local business support organization to see what is offered there.

2. Hire a professional who can help out for those aspects of your work. If the skills you need are more about the business of what you do, and less about the actual advocacy work, you might do better to find someone to help. An accountant, or a lawyer, or a virtual assistant[9] can handle some of the business and administrative work that you don't want to tackle.

3. If you need to brush up on the advocacy skills themselves, volunteering can help fill some of the gaps. If you think you want to help cancer patients, for example, then contact the local breast cancer organization, or the Leukemia Lymphoma Society – or any cancer related organization where you can learn on the (volunteer) job. (However, see the sidebar about volunteer work in Chapter Eight.)

4. Much of the information you need to fill your business-knowledge gaps can be found in this book; or, if it's not here, then the resources you need are listed in footnotes or the Resources section in the back of this book. Sometimes all you really need to know is what questions to ask, then you can ask others to fill in the blanks for you.

---

8   Find overviews and student ratings at www.HealthAdvocatePrograms.com.

9   More information about Virtual Assistants can be found in the Resources Section at the end of this book .

5. Join one of the professional organizations focused on health advocacy. From business skills to advocacy skills, networking and more, these organizations offer support and education to private, independent advocates.[10]

What About Certification and Licensing for Advocates?

Not a week goes by that someone doesn't send me an email, or leave a phone message, asking me how they can become certified to be a patient or health advocate.

And I can understand why. Most health-related professionals who work directly with patients have some sort of certification, degree program, board membership, and/or licensing they must obtain. That's the admission price for applying for a job, and being hired into a health career.

But not so for health or patient advocacy – at least not yet.

Private advocacy, as a professional career where people have set up practices and delivered services, is only a few years old. Individuals started offering these kinds of services as early as 2000 or 2001, but it has only been since about 2009 that they began networking with others and working to formalize the kinds of practices you're reading out in this book, or that you'll encounter in the marketplace.

What that means is that the profession hasn't been a profession long enough to have established any criteria that is nationally, or internationally, recognized – no formal credential that consistently means the same thing in either the United States or Canada.

Yes, there are a number of educational organizations offering programs, some excellent, that provide a certificate to those who complete their courses. Those are local-to-that-institution certifications. They are not nationally recognized.

Licensing is a similar story. Licenses are bestowed by the state or province one resides in. Like a plumber, or a hairdresser, or a pharmacist, or a nurse, professionals apply for licenses, and if they meet the state's criteria, that state will provide a license.

But states license professions based on the standards developed by credentialing organizations, and advocacy has no such organization. A handful of professional advocacy organizations are in the process of studying possibilities, and it is anticipated that sometime in the next five years or so, an agreed-upon credential may exist.

But today, no such certification or license exists. Therefore – no – you do not need to be certified, nor licensed, to be a private professional patient or health advocate.

What Educational Programs Are Available?

The Internet, advocacy organizations, other advocates and advisors, and the government can provide you with every piece of knowledge, or every resource, you could possibly need to be sure you have all the details you need to start your advocacy practice.

None of this work is rocket science. Private advocacy is just a new way of offering assistance to patients and caregivers. People have been starting businesses and they have been advocating for friends and loved ones for centuries, or longer. So none of what you need to do or learn is hidden or mysterious.

But sometimes, because it's so new, it's not obvious. And because we have a few years of professional development under our belts, sometimes resources exist that you wouldn't necessarily know about unless you were already networking with others who are pursuing a practice, too.

Here is a list of the kinds of resources that may help fill your knowledge gaps. A master list of specific resources for each of these categories can be found in the Resources section in the back of this book, and on the book's website at: www.HealthAdvocateResources.com.

1. Business assistance from government organizations like the Small Business Administration, or SCORE (Service Corps of Retired Executives), SBDC (Small Business Development Center) or CBN (Canada Business Network).

2. Advocacy degree and certificate programs from more than two dozen educational institutions and organizations.[10]

3. Membership organizations that support both the advocacy work itself and business support for advocates[10].

4. Networking, either face-to-face networking at conferences and meetings, or through online Forums such as those at LinkedIn. These may include advocacy focused opportunities, or local events put on by your local Chamber of Commerce or business networking organizations.

5. Volunteer opportunities cover the healthcare gamut, including places with people who need your help like community health centers, senior centers and churches or synagogues.

6. This book and *The Health Advocate's Marketing Handbook*.

---

10   Find a master list of all education programs , events and organizations at www.HealthAdvocatePrograms.com

Chapter Six
Brass Tacks:
The Business of Being in Business

There will be many times (as you get started, probably the majority of the time) when being in the health advocacy business will be less about providing health advocacy services, and more about the business of being in business.

These kinds of details often stymie advocates who just don't know where to start to put themselves into business. It's the paralysis that results from not knowing the answers because you don't even know the questions.

So here are the questions, along with an explanation of why the question is important, some ways to answer them for yourself, and resources to assist in your answer and decision-making.

Sometimes we can't make these decisions without other experts to help us. You may need to consult with an attorney, an accountant, a CPA, a marketing specialist, a business advisor or even the loved one you share a bank account with. In some cases, consulting with your crystal ball will be just as useful. And sometimes your own preferences, with no other input, will be all the support you need.

As you make your way through each of these questions, you'll want to have your Workbook handy. It will supply additional resources to help you answer the questions, make your decisions, and record your own answers.

TASK #6

The basics of being in business are important details at the outset of your planning because they will give structure to every other business decision you make.

As you review each question,
record your decisions or additional questions in the Workbook.

Important Business Details – Questions to Consider

Here is the list of questions that are addressed in this chapter. Of course, they aren't all the business decisions you'll be making. Many others will be tackled in subsequent chapters. But these will get you off to a good start. Each is necessary to make before you actually hang out your "I'm really in business now" shingle.

A.   **What type of business formation will you choose?**

B.   **What is your exit strategy? How will you go out of business?**

C.   **What will you name your business?**

D.   **What licenses and identifications will you need?**

E.   **Where will your office(s) be located?**

F.   **What will your geographic reach be?**

G.   **Will you hire help?**

H.   **Who can provide you with advice when you need it?**

I.   **How will you handle money and transactions?**

J.   **What communications tools will you use?**

K.   **How will you get around? What transportation will you need?**

L.   **What kinds of insurance will you need?**

Let's get started. It's time to do some business decision-making!

A. What type of business formation will you choose?

Who Can Help	Other Decisions This Will Affect	Cost Considerations	Priority
• A business attorney • Online legal assistance • The SBA, SCORE SBDC, CBN [11]	• Your business name • Bank Accounts • IRS or CRA • Local licensing • Insurance	Will depend on your choice of formation.	Top priority (because so many other decisions rest on your choice)

---

11 Find more information about the SBA (Small Business Administration), SCORE (Service Corps of Retired Executives) and SBDC (Small Business Development Center) iand CBN (Canada Business Network) n the Resources section in the back of this book.

Business formation is a question better answered with the help of an attorney rather than simply trying to sort it out yourself. It may have bigger ramifications about who owns your business, what kind of insurance or business license you'll need, what your tax status and liability are, what formal meetings and documentation must take place, and more. Further, each state has different descriptions and requirements for these formations.

Your first decision will be: do you want to be a for-profit company? Or would you prefer to set up a non-profit organization? (See the sidebar on page 55 to help you make this decision.)

Should you determine you want to establish a for-profit business, here are the basic types of business formations from which you can choose. Remember, different states and provinces may call them something different, but the basic formations will be the same.

Sole Proprietorship

This is the simplest type of business to own and run, and requires only that you file some paperwork with your state to register your business name. (Some states don't even require that much.) Pro: easy Cons: may have insurance and liability ramifications, and may mean you'll take personal losses if you are ever sued.

Partnership

You and at least one other person contract to be co-owners of your business, meaning you incur all the costs and liabilities together, and you reap the benefits and rewards together, too. Like a sole proprietorship, you may not need to file government paperwork, but you will want to make sure any agreements you make are in writing, agreed upon and signed by all partners. Pros: easy, and a good way to spread out the liabilities. Cons: many a good friendship and business was ruined by a partnership that didn't work out when workloads were perceived to be different, or money wasn't spent wisely by the other partner.

LLC: a Limited Liability Company

An LLC is a state-designated formation that can be entered into by an individual, or a group of partners, and limits their liability in some of the same ways corporations do. The key to LLCs is to make sure all funding is kept separate from personal funding (when you make enough money, you pay yourself a paycheck, for example). Some formal paperwork is required, like an operating agreement. Pro: a fairly simple way to get most of the protection a corporation provides. Con: may require state taxes and paperwork that a sole proprietorship or partnership do not require.

PLLC: a Professional Limited Liability Company

A PLLC is also a state-designated formation for licensed professionals. The keyword here is "licensed" – so if you are licensed as a doctor or a nurse or another form of licensing, you'll want to review whether this is a possibility, or even a necessity, for your new business. Like choosing an LLC, your decision will have business licensing, tax and liability considerations. Pros and Cons are the same as for an LLC with the exception of possible malpractice, which is not protected by a PLLC.

LLP: is a Limited Liability Partnership

Very similar to an LLC, an LLP is formed for service organizations where the partners do not want to be responsible for the other partners' obligations or debts which could arise from negligence, misconduct or malpractice. Forming an LLP, like these other business formations, requires the paperwork be solid and agreed upon to be sure those obligations are spelled out and that all partners are in agreement. The pros and cons are the same as for LLCs.

Corporation

Corporations are set up specifically to protect those people who form them, and/or to allow others to buy in to that business entity as investors. When a corporation is formed, it creates what is called the "corporate veil," meaning, in effect, a way to protect those individuals who have formed it. It becomes its own entity, separate from any individuals, which means it will have its own name, its own bank accounts, its own insurance and more. Two main types of corporations may be created, one called an "S" Corp, the other a "C" Corp. Consult your attorney if you are interested in creating a corporation.

DBA or Fictitious Business Name

(See later in this Chapter: *What Will You Name Your Business?*)

In Canada you'll find additional corporate structures for cooperatives and societies (non-profits). Both of these structures will require legal counsel for you to determine if they are right for you.

Should I Set up My Business as a Non-Profit?

Besides the fact that very few of us actually make a profit in the first few years of business (making us all non-profits for awhile!) you may want to consider forming a legal non-profit entity by choice.

As individual health advocates there are three approaches you can use to make this decision. One is based on how you will choose to bring in your money. The second is based on who will be in charge. The third is based on how you plan to exit your new business entity.

A non-profit organization is one that exists because of its mission, whereas a for-profit business exists to do just that – make a profit. For example, a non-profit may exist to help people who don't have health insurance find proper medical care at no cost to them for that assistance. The for-profit business parallel might charge people a sum of money to help them find that same kind of proper medical care instead of providing it for free. The non-profit has a mission of helping people regardless of ability to pay. The for-profit business has a goal of helping those who can afford its services.

But of course, nothing is really free, so even when services are provided for "free," there is a cost to providing that "free" help. Money must still be brought into the organization. So, instead of collecting money from clients as a for-profit business would do, a non-profit might instead apply for grants from the government, or from individuals, or from health-related foundations that make such grants.

A for-profit business is run by a president or a CEO, or the owner – which might all be the same person. As the owner of a for-profit business, you might well have paid or unpaid advisors, but all the final decisions are yours to make. Those decisions include who gets paid how much.

Further, if the for-profit business brings in extra money, then the business must also pay taxes on that extra – the profit.

Contrast the one-person decision-maker, taxpaying model with the way non-profits make decisions and payment to their workers. That is, they must have a board of trustees who make the major decisions for how the non-profit will manage its business needs, including the determination of how much each paycheck will be. Non-profits must budget and spend all their earned income in any given year, so if plenty of money comes in, then that money must be spent, too, and there will be nothing left that can be taxed. On the other hand, if not much money comes in, then there's nothing left to spend, or to increase paychecks with either.

Finally, if you, as the initiator of an organization, plan to sell the organization / business when you're ready to do something else (like retire or change careers) then your only choice is a for-profit business. Non-profits cannot be sold as a business (although their assets can be sold for the benefit of the organization.)

If you think establishing a non-profit is a good choice for you, consult with an attorney who has experience in filing the necessary paperwork. Non-profits have very strict rules and guidelines for their establishment and their annual reporting.

B. What is your exit strategy? How will you go out of business?

Who Can Help	Other Decisions This Will Affect	Cost Considerations	Priority
• A business advisor • This book • The SBA, SCORE or SBDC	• Business formation • Your business name • Your accounting and bookkeeping	Time only, as you consider options	Top priority – read the reasons next

You're probably rubbing your eyes, or wondering if somehow the pages in this book are out of order. Why on earth would the second decision you need to make be to determine how you will go out of business?

But yes, there is a method to my business-ending-question madness.

When you gave thought to your goals in Chapter Three, you were asked about your reasons for being in business for yourself. Among the reasons you declared may have been the fact that you aren't quite ready to retire, so health advocacy is something you can do on your own timetable. Or maybe you are hoping to build a business where others will do the actual work while you manage it. Maybe you're hoping to fund your retirement by selling your health advocacy business.

When you put your goals together with the question of how you will go out of business, you'll understand the bearing those two decisions will have on the next several considerations in this chapter.

Some business-ending options to consider:

♦ You can go out of business just by no longer taking on new clients and phasing out the work you have with current clients. In that case, you'll simply handle your business the way you want to handle it, without regard to someone else taking it over one day.

♦ You can go out of business by selling your practice to someone else. If you hope to do that one day, then it will affect many of the decisions you make as you go along. For example, it will affect how you do all your accounting, how solidly you build your brand, how extensive your resource database will be, how broad your clientele is, and more.

♦ You can go out of business by going bankrupt.

Which way do you hope to go out of business? Just what is your exit strategy? Keep it in mind as you make other going-into-business decisions.

C. What will you name your business?

Who Can Help	Other Decisions This Will Affect	Cost Considerations	Priority
• An attorney • A marketer • The SBA, SCORE or SBDC	• Bank accounts • IRS tax status • Local licensing • Insurance	Time only	Top priority – so many other decisions rest on this choice

Naming your business is more difficult than naming your children, but must be done perfectly for the same reason: it will represent your business for the rest of its life.

No pressure or anything.

Here are some considerations for naming your business:

♦ It must be easy to remember.

♦ It must represent what you do. Don't make it too general because it won't represent anything. "ABC Enterprises" is way too general. But don't make it too specific, either, because someday you may want to expand beyond your initial goals and services. "Joanie's Poison Ivy Rash Advocacy" is just too specific.

♦ There are great words that represent advocacy like "navigation" or "directions." There are other words that represent geography like "of Colorado" or "of Pensacola" and as long as you don't plan to expand your geography, they work well.

♦ It must be available and easily translated into a URL (Uniform Resource Locator) – your website name. If you try to use a very generic name, including the word "advocates" in it, then you'll have some difficulty unless you add your geography or another word to it, because most of those good names seem to be taken. www.PatientAdvocatesofTimbuktu.com might be available. But www.PatientAdvocates.com is already established by someone else.

Considering using your own name? Joan's Advocacy Enterprises is easy and represents what you do, but what if you decide to sell your practice later, or turn it over to a business partner sometime in the future? Using your personal name as part of your business name can actually diminish its value. (Which is one of the reasons you needed to think about how you will go out of business. See? Some method to my madness.)

It's entirely possible to use two real business names, if you choose. One might be your official corporate name while the other is what is called a "DBA," which means "Doing Business As" also called a Fictitious Business Name.

For example, I have one large corporate name for my businesses – DiagKNOWsis. Few people recognize that name even though it's on my tax filings and bank account. But people do recognize AdvoConnection, and Every Patient's Advocate. This book is published by DiagKNOWsis Media. Those are names I use for my branding (a marketing term – see Chapter Nine.) In some of my outreach I'll use the names together, like "AdvoConnection, one of the DiagKNOWsis Family of Patient Empowerment and Advocacy Activities".

If you want to use a DBA, you'll need to file paperwork to do so, which notifies the state (or province) and the public that your business or corporate name is different from the name the public will grow to recognize.

Spend some time, and talk to others, about possible names for your business. Try several on for size. Check to see if the URL is something you can live with. (You can find tools for figuring out what URLs may be available in the Resources section in the back of this book.)

Once you arrive at your choice, it will fit like a glove. It will produce one of those "aha!" moments in your life.

And that's the point, too, where the possibility of going into business for yourself will truly feel as if it's taking shape.

D. What licenses and identifications will you need?

Who Can Help	Other Decisions This Will Affect	Cost Considerations	Priority
• Your county clerk • The IRS website • Dun & Bradstreet	• Bank accounts • IRS tax status • Insurance • Your business name • Your office location	Time There will be some fees for some licensing	Top priority – so many other decisions rest on this choice

(Note: This section refers to business licensing only, and not to advocate licensing – because there are no licenses needed for advocates. See page 49.)

Your location, your business formation, your bookkeeping and taxes, even your ability to work from home if you choose, will all require, or be dependent on some of the licenses and identification numbers you'll need to obtain. The list isn't long, nor are they difficult to come by. But your official existence as a legal entity – in other words, staying on the right side of the law – might be.

Requirements for these vary from locale to locale, state to state, province to province, and country to country. For each license number or ID you obtain, ask if the person who helps you knows of others you need. (For example, your county clerk will know if your state or province requires anything else.)

Here are some of the official licenses and identifications you may need, and a resource for how to obtain them:

United States

Local, county or state business licenses: Since each state and/or locale has different business licensing requirements, these will vary from advocate to advocate. If you are in the United States, figuring out what business licenses you may need is very simple. Go to the SBA website (Small Business Administration) at: http://www.sba.gov/licenses-and-permits and input your zip code, choose "General Licensing" and voila! Your list of necessary licenses.

There are many other details listed there, too. And no, you don't have to have everything listed in place to get your business going. However, you may want to bookmark this page, because there is great information here to cover many of the business details you will need over time, not just to get this list of licenses.

Employer Identification Number (EIN): One of the questions advocates ask is, if they don't plan to hire other people, do they really need an employer ID? The answer is yes – and here's why.

If you set yourself up as a corporation, or, in some states, an LLC or other semi-corporate structure, an EIN will be a must-have.

But even if you set yourself up as a sole proprietor or partnership, an employer ID will stand in for your social security number. Anyone who pays you, like clients, or clients' attorneys, or organizations that might hire you to speak – may ask you for your social security number or EIN. Since good practice means you want to protect your social security number, just use your EIN which doesn't incur the same nightmares if someone chooses to use it as a result of identity theft.

Another crucial number will be your state's tax ID number. Even if no state sales tax is collected for your work (most states have no tax on services or intangible goods), you want to be sure to get ahold of one of these numbers. You might need one someday, and by obtaining one early on, you show your state, in good faith, that you are following the laws. You may also be asked to file a sales tax return quarterly or annually, but if you've collected no tax, you just send it back showing that you've collected no tax.

DUNS Number: If you ever plan to apply for a grant from the United States federal government, they will require you to have a DUNS number (Data Universal Numbering System) which helps them track how federal grant money is allocated.

If you are forming a non-profit organization (see page 55) then you should probably apply for a DUNS number right away. Otherwise, this is not a necessary step since you can apply later for a DUNS number should the opportunity to apply for a grant arise.

If or when you decide you need one, DUNS numbers are supplied by Dun & Bradstreet. They are free to obtain, and are instantaneous when you apply by phone. Call 1-866-705-5711.

Canada

Local, county or province business licences: Each Canadian province and locale has its own requirements just like states and locales in the US do. Unfortunately there does not appear to be a nationwide search available for finding a list of licences needed.

But it is still fairly easy to get the information you need. Simply search using the name of your city or province, and "business licence". Your search results will yield the name of the licensing authority in your area, and your list of necessary business licences will be found in there.

Industry Codes – US and Canada

The last number you may need to be concerned with in both countries is your industry code which is used usually by taxing authorities, but may also be used if you apply for business loans.

In the United States, the industry code you'll need is called an SIC code (Standard Industrial Classification), although SICs are in the process of being replaced by NAIC codes (North American Industry Classification).

Canadian and American businesses both use NAICs. The best code for general advocacy services is 624100.

In Canada, the Canada Revenue Agency oversees industry codes. You can find the agency's website here: http://www.cra-arc.gc.ca For general advocacy services, the best code seems to be the same as the NAICs code: Individual and Family Services – 624100

Your attorney or CPA may be able to help you determine the right code for your business.

E. Where will your office(s) be located?

Who Can Help	Other Decisions This Will Affect	Cost Considerations	Priority
• Your significant other • Leasing agent	• Anything that requires your office address • Who else can use your space	• Rent • Taxes	Medium

The decision about where your office (and business) will be located isn't as simple as one might think. There are actually a number of considerations related to space, your attention span, and your ability to afford space outside your home.

Will you work from home? Or will you find that office space located elsewhere is a wiser choice? These questions should help you determine the right answer for you:

How well can you focus on your work?

It can be very distracting working from home! If you have kids or pets or chatty neighbors, or if your gardening or a good book or favorite TV show are irresistible, then you won't be a good candidate for working from home.

On the other hand, if you are able to self-direct yourself, and can focus on your work to the exclusion of all those tempting, or irritating, outside influences, then working from home is not only a luxury (yes – like me – you, too, can work in your jammies) but it's a money-saver, too.

Can you walk away from your work?

This is the opposite of the question above. If, like many entrepreneurs, you are a workaholic, love what you do, and have trouble pulling away from your workday, then working from home may not be all it's cracked up to be.

Balance is important, so unless you have the ability to shut down your computer and walk away, then you might do better to rent space somewhere else so that you close and lock the door at an appointed hour each day, go home and, well, be balanced.

Of course, as an advocate, and assuming you'll spend plenty of time in person with clients and potential clients, walking away from your office (no matter where it is located) will be a part of most days anyway.

Can you afford office rent?

The right answer for your office location may actually be decided by the cost of rent. Depending on where you live, you may find possibilities that are very inexpensive ($200 a month) or quite expensive ($1000+ per month.)

There are two great scenarios in many locations that offer low monthly costs with additional business assistance.

1. In some cities you'll find "business incubators" which are low rent and housed along with other small businesses. Sometimes they also offer business advisors to help you. These business incubators are sometimes sponsored by universities, or a chamber of commerce, or local community college. If an incubator is of interest to you, phone the "small business" office of any of those organizations and ask. If they aren't the right resource, they'll let you know who is.

2. The second great scenario is often called an "executive suites" arrangement. Other names include "instant offices" or "temp offices." These situations offer a small individual space, very inexpensively, and shared conference rooms, copy machines, Internet access, maybe even a receptionist and other attributes.

Who else will need to use your space?

There may be others who you'll need to share your space with. Employees, freelancer/ independent contractors, potential clients, current clients and others may need to meet with you in your space, so the location you choose needs to account for others, too.

If you decide to work from home, it won't preclude meeting with others. You can always meet with other folks in a local coffee shop, or a Panera (a personal favorite).

If you want to offer meeting space with some sense of privacy, you'll want to think seriously about finding office space. It will make you appear more business-like too.

Considerations for Office Space

If you decide to get new space, you'll have decisions about furniture, signage, mail delivery and others to make. Do yourself a favor and don't spend any more money than necessary on the niceties and extras until you know you've got money coming in. It's so tempting! But it may tempt you right out of business as you struggle to pay your bills.

Considerations for Working from Home

You won't need fancy signs or fancy furniture, but there are some considerations for setting up your office at home.

First – you'll want to keep your location private. Since you'll be dealing with the public, and since people's lives and money will be in your hands, your mere existence at an identifiable address will invite some people to violate your privacy. (I say this from personal experience, by the way.)

To keep your location / home private, rent a post office box for your mail, and use that address in all your materials and on your website. If the post office isn't convenient, there are stores like Mailboxes Plus or UPS Stores that offer private boxes for your mail. They will cost $100 or more per year, but the privacy is worth it.

Second, make sure your work space is separated in some way from the rest of your home – for two reasons.

1. When tax time comes, you'll meet the requirements for a home office. If you set up your dining room as your office, that's great – but don't use it as a dining room, too. If you set up your guestroom as your home office, be sure your guests sleep elsewhere. You can cordon off a section of a bedroom, or set up a corner of your basement or attic. Just keep it separated. Once it's set up, take photos of your space to show that it's separate, just in case you have to prove it to the IRS or CRA (Canadian Revenue Agency) one day.

2. A separated space creates a barrier and a reminder. If there are others in your household (a spouse or partner, children, and yes, even the family dog) then it becomes too easy to interrupt you, or make noises during important business phone calls. Imagine pouring your heart out to an advocate about your recent terminal diagnosis, only to have that advocate start yelling at the kids to "keep it down!" in the middle of your story. Don't be that advocate!

F. What will your geographic reach be?

Who Can Help	Other Decisions This Will Affect	Cost Considerations	Priority
• Other advocates • The SBA, SCORE or SBDC	• Marketing • Phone number choices • Education choices: state laws • licensing	• Travel costs	Medium

The reason this decision is important at this time is because some of your other decisions will rest on your geography choices. For example, if you don't intend to work outside your own local area, then you can use just a local phone number. But if your reach is broader, you may decide you'll need a toll-free number. Marketing decisions will also rest on your decision: everything from the key words you use in your website, to your brochure distribution. In addition, if you plan to work in states other than your own, you'll need to be sure you are familiar with any state laws that affect delivery of healthcare, licensing or how insurance works.

Here are some questions that will help you make your geographic reach decisions a little clearer:

- **Your services – do you need to offer them in person, or can you handle them by phone and email?**

   If you are a medical billing advocate, you know you don't need to meet with clients in person. But if you are a hospital bedside advocate then you'll need to be in the same location as your client.

   Even if your services require you to be in the same geographic area, you may be able to accomplish that if you can travel to the client's location. That will require your client to pay for your travel, though. While some clients may be willing to pay for your travel, most, in these early stages of advocacy as a profession, will not.

   And don't forget, you might find a fellow advocate in another location that you can partner with as a subcontractor.

- **Are you a licensed medical professional in a specific state or province?**

   If you are a doctor, nurse, NP or other licensed medical professional, you may be restricted to working in the state or province you are licensed and/or insured in.

   So far as I know, there is no blanket "one size fits all" answer to the question about whether licensed professionals can cross state lines. To this point, in conversations with licensed professionals all over the country, the answers are not clear. It seems to depend on who the question is asked of (a lawyer? A state bureaucrat?) and even then, the answers seem to vary.

   If you are a licensed medical professional, and your intent is to operate outside your own state as a health advocate (meaning you will not be performing medical tasks or making medical decisions) you will want to ask your lawyer, your insurer, and your licensing body for their opinions.

G. Will you hire help?

Who Can Help	Other Decisions This Will Affect	Cost Considerations	Priority
• Other advocates • Service Professionals • The SBA, SCORE or SBDC	• Workload • Business decisions	• Salaries and benefits • Cost of services	Medium

When you first start your advocacy business, you may be the Jack or Jill of all trades regarding your business tasks, but you may soon learn that it's almost impossible to keep up with everything – and do it well.

There are some tasks you won't be able to do without help. You won't be able to issue yourself a license, or file your legal corporate papers. But the majority of business tasks aren't difficult, nor are they difficult to learn, so it's worthwhile for you to give them a try, at least as you get started.

By trying them yourself, you'll soon learn what you want to offload-er-delegate to someone else. For example, marketing tasks can be a real pain unless you understand and love to market yourself. (Learn more about this in *The Health Advocate's Marketing Handbook* – find discounts for the book in the Resources section.)

There are other people who would love to be hired to help you. In particular, hiring another professional is one great way to fill those gaps you identified in Chapter Five. Further, it's the way you grow your business if you find you have too many clients and not enough hours in your day.

There are two ways to engage others to help you. You might hire them as employees, or as independent contractors.

You are probably most familiar with an employee-type relationship. In that relationship the parameters such as where the work will be done, and time (work hours and amount of time), are directed by the employer.

Independent contractors have a different relationship with the person who hires them. You may have heard them called "subcontractors" and "freelancers" too. (See page 45 for more about contractor relationships.)

Independent contractors are hired more on a project basis, with no ongoing relationship once the project is finished, unless you hire them to do another project later. The person who hires them is not allowed, by IRS or CRA rules, to dictate where the work will be done, or what hours are required, among other criteria.

There are real benefits and detriments to hiring either employees or independent contractors. For example, it may seem great to have an employee who does what you need him to do, when you need him to do it. But you'll be responsible for providing his paycheck even before your provide your own, and you'll share his tax liability, plus other possible benefits like health insurance, sick leave, vacations and more.

At least at first, an independent contractor may fit your hiring capabilities more closely. Just be aware that you'll be constrained by IRS and CRA rules regarding your control over their work. You may also have some tax withholding requirements, depending on the contractor you hire.

It would be impossible to help you make your decisions about the best way to engage others to help you because every advocate business owner's needs are different. Instead I'll refer you to your local SBA, SCORE or SBA office and suggest you ask them to walk you through the best solutions for making your help-hiring decisions.

H. Who can provide you with advice when you need it?

Who Can Help	Other Decisions This Will Affect	Cost Considerations	Priority
• Business advisors, mentors, attorneys, CPAs, coaches, other advocates, others	Any decisions that will benefit by someone else's input	Depends on the advice you seek and your relationship with the person providing it.	Medium

No matter how smart you are about business, having experts to consult with on a regular basis can be a huge benefit to you.

All businesses, no matter how large or small, need to find experts in the aspects of business they are not well-suited to handling. An accountant or CPA will be invaluable when it comes to budgeting, and certainly when it comes time to tracking expenses for tax purposes.

An attorney will be valuable for helping you establish contracts with clients or subcontractors, or to develop disclaimers about your work – in effect – keeping you out of hot water.

You can either choose to have a very formal advisor relationship, such as a Board of Trustees (for a non-profit – see Sidebar on page 55) or a Board of Directors (for a corporation.) Or it can be less formal, by tapping into help only when you need it.

The key is how decision-making responsibilities are established. If you expect your experts / advisors to make decisions for you about how you will run your organization, and you depend on them for those decisions, then you'll want a more formal "Board" structure that spells out exactly what those responsibilities and expectations are. Board decisions often create a fiduciary relationship; that is, those advisors are making money-related decisions for you.

Less formal, but no less informative and helpful, might be a mentor or coach who can help you make decisions for moving your business forward when those decisions need to be made. Included here are the SBA, SCORE, CBN or your local SBDC. And don't forget networking groups, even online forums where you can ask other advocates about the choices they made and their subsequent experiences with those decisions.[12]

Putting a formal Board in place will be necessary for several of the more structured business formations described in Section A earlier in this chapter.

I. How will you handle money and transactions?

Who Can Help	Other Decisions This Will Affect	Cost Considerations	Priority
• Local or online banker • Online sites like Paypal, Google Wallet, Square or Pay Simple	Administrative	Depends on the service	Medium

Money! It's the root of all business, because no matter how philanthropic your goals are for being in business, if you can't support the cost of doing business, then you won't be in business for long.

There are three categories of money handling: bringing it in, spending it, and managing it while we've got it.

Managing Business Money

Even if you are a sole practitioner who, legally, can mix your personal and business funds, it's wise to set up a bank account in your business's name with you as the main signer on the account. In order to do so, you'll need your business license, your business name, and you may need your taxpayer ID or Social Security number. (Now you understand why those are higher up our list of business decisions.)

Look for a bank or credit union that is willing to give you a free checking account, even though you are a business. Sometimes local institutions offer free accounts (as opposed to

---

12   Find a list of known online forums and discussion groups in the Resources.

larger banks with locations in many cities or states.) If you think you may need a business loan at some point in the future, these smaller banks and credit unions are often good options, too. If you are female, you'll find some of the larger banks have entire departments focused on enticing woman-owned businesses. You may also want to find one that allows online bill paying (it's very convenient and easy).

I use an online bank that offers free checking (I'm a sole practitioner), and in order to make deposits, I take a photo of the check with my smartphone. Seriously easy.

To open your account, you can "loan" yourself a few hundred dollars. Make yourself a note to pay yourself back later, once you begin bringing in money from clients.

If you open a corporate business account, your bank will have state laws it needs to adhere to, so some of the rules may vary.

Once you have your bank account in place, get set up with a bookkeeping system. You may want to check with a CPA or an accountant who will know some of the best management tools for business bookkeeping like Quicken, QuickBooks or Freshbooks.

It's most important to track every piece of financial information that will affect your taxes. As a business owner you'll find that almost every penny you spend for your business is deductible, but some of those expenses are more or less deductible than others. The important thing at this point is just to keep track – thus the initial set up with an accountant or CPA.

Collecting Money

Making it easy for clients to pay you is the focus when it comes to setting up the ways you can collect what you are owed.

Cash may be king, but it will be a rare experience to have your client pay you cash. So instead we need to look at other possibilities and ways of collecting money.

You are more likely to be paid with a check (or money order) or by credit card.

If they pay you using a check, then you will want to make sure the check clears before you deliver your services to them. Now, I'm telling you this, and you're reading it, and yet I guarantee you that someday you will accept a check and deliver your services only to find out later that the check bounced. I can't tell you how many times I have been floored to learn that I have accepted a check, and delivered a copy of my book, only to have to "threaten" someone later if they don't make the check good. Only twice have I ultimately been stiffed. That's two times too many. It's frustrating and insulting.

And then there are credit cards. For advocacy services, in particular those that do not require you to meet in-person, the ability to accept credit cards is a must.

The basics of being a credit card "merchant" (accepting credit cards) are this: When you, as the merchant, accept a credit card, the acceptance system you use will collect the money from the client's credit card company, and deposit that collected money to your bank account (or to an account you have with them, then you make a withdrawal from that account) – minus the fees they charge. Some require a monthly base fee be paid, no matter how much you use their services, plus a percentage of the money collected. Others charge a percentage plus a per-transaction fee. Since they charge no base fee, that percentage may be a bit higher.

Some advocates want to set up a "shopping cart" system on their websites which is a good, but expensive system. Shopping carts usually require you to commit to a monthly fee for their use, plus a percentage of the amount charged. So before you even take in your first dollar every month, it may cost you $35 or more, then another 2-3 % of each dollar thereafter.

You might choose, instead, to use a vendor system like Paypal or Pay Simple. Using these kinds of services requires only that you link to them from your own website, or that you issue an invoice from their website. Until you are at the point where you are bringing in $10,000 or more per month, these services are probably less expensive than using your own shopping cart. Your webmaster will be able to incorporate them into your site.

If you'd like to accept credit cards in person, you can do that easily and inexpensively using a smartphone. Paypal, Square, Intuit and others offer little gizmos that insert into the audio jack of your smartphone. You set up the transaction, then swipe your client's credit card through the gizmo. He signs for the transaction using his index finger on the smartphone screen – and there you go. All paid.

If you find much of your work is taking place by phone, and not in person, then you may need a payment solution that allows your client to verbally provide her credit card number. Many older people don't use the Internet, and some people are reticent to use a credit card number online. If you won't see your client in person to swipe a card, and can't wait for a check to arrive in the mail, then you'll want to have the capability to accept credit card information by phone. Paypal and Pay Simple offer this capability. There may be additional fees, so be sure to read any contracts or terms of service you're asked to agree to.

A note about choosing the best credit card service for you: Do your due diligence for selecting the right credit card vendor to work with by comparing those fees and researching customer satisfaction. Depending on the fee structure, you may find that for every $100 your client pays you, you get to keep only $90 – or $97.50 – or anything in between. You might also want to do a web search for user reviews to see if they perform as promised. Remember, their marketing promises, and their actual service delivery may vary.

(Note: we'll cover how to price your services in Chapter Eight.)

Spending Business Money

There are a variety of reasons and ways your money will be spent. You'll be paying other people for their help, you'll be buying office supplies, you may pay rent, you'll have to put gas in your car, you'll be taking potential clients to lunch and more.

Keep every receipt, every piece of proof you spent the money on a business-related transaction. It's also best to at least keep them all in one place. For example, I have a bin in my office where I file receipts as I collect them based on which tax deduction category they fall under. You can ask your CPA to help you set up a similar system. Or, you can just throw all your business receipts into a shoebox. Just keep them in one place.

One of the easiest ways to keep track is by consistently using a business credit card. You may decide to apply for a new card, using your business name, or you may just decide to devote one of the personal cards you already have to business expenses only. If you have incorporated, you'll need to apply for a corporate card. You may find the expenses involved, like annual fees or interest rates, may be higher.

Some of the business credit card companies will issue you a statement at the end of the year that reports all your expenditures by categories to help you with your taxes.

When you pay other people, you'll need to track the money differently because, as mentioned previously, there will be tax ramifications according to their relationship with you (employee vs independent contractor.) You'll get involved in issuing end-of-the-fiscal year statements to them, plus additional schedules in your tax returns. These will vary by state, province or country, so consult with your accountant.

J. What communications tools will you use?

Who Can Help	Other Decisions This Will Affect	Cost Considerations	Priority
• Phone, Internet companies • Webmasters • Email companies	• All other communications decisions • All marketing decisions	Depends on the service and the equipment	High

Your communications tools will be like running shoes are to a marathoner, or a camera is to a photographer – you'll use them and depend on them constantly, every day, for almost every important task.

These tools are among the most important investments you'll make, and are therefore worthy of spending extra for top quality, high end equipment and services.

A good computer, fast, consistent Internet access, a business phone (wireless or land line), a fax machine (or fax software on your high end computer), good email management software (Outlook, Thunderbird or others), possibly a toll free phone number, and others.

Your specific needs may vary, so here are some general considerations to review before you invest in these important tools:

Dedication: When it comes time to do your taxes, you'll need to be able to state what percent of your tool cost was dedicated to business use. Now, if you decide to use a cell phone as your business phone, and only once-in-a-blue-moon do you make a personal call from that phone, then it will have been 100% dedicated to business use. Likewise if you never use your computer except for business, you'll be able to deduct 100% of its purchase price, including software, plus 100% of your Internet cost.

But I suspect it's a rare advocate who never uses her computer or cell phone for personal reasons. So keep in mind that you'll just need to track your usage somehow, so you'll have the right information when it comes to tax time.

I mention this here because, since you know you'll be able to deduct these expenses from your taxes, you might decide to invest in better quality tools. I'm not suggesting you splurge on all the latest toys. But knowing Uncle Sam will help you pay for them may give you a bit more flexibility.

Portability: If you'll be spending much of your time out of your office, perhaps calling on potential clients, or in meetings, or sitting by the bedside in the hospital, then you'll want to think about portability for your phone and computer, too. A lighter weight computer is easier to carry around. A tablet or iPad might even work for you.

As for a phone number, you may want to get a cell phone that will allow you to keep your phone number no matter where you move to, anywhere in your country. A landline phone number may have to be changed if you choose to move elsewhere.

Phone and Fax Considerations: If your wireless phone will be your business phone, then you'll want to be sure you choose a wireless service that has high quality coverage in the entire area your business will reach. The last thing you want to do is drop a call from a potential client! If you spend much of your time in your office, or you have the liberty to phone clients long after they have left a message, then a landline will provide better call quality. Of course, you can have both, using one for your business phone number, but forwarding to the other when it's more convenient.

Fax and Toll Free systems are available online, inexpensively. Faxes can be delivered to your computer through email, and you can even send them by scanning them and attaching them to an email or letting your computer dial a fax number. Toll free phone numbers are available for taking messages. You then phone back the person who left the message. (Find some of these resources for both kinds of services in the Resources section at the end of this book.)

Email Considerations: Choose a business email address that isn't tied to the company you get your Internet service from because someday you may not use that same Internet service provider. For example, if you use a Verizon or Comcast email address, and later move to another location, or decide to save money using a different service, you'll lose access to that email address, and will have to expend time, resources and money to change your email address for every current client, potential client, colleague, website registration, and all your marketing materials.

Instead, use an email address that will never change, no matter what other changes may take place. Your own web domain is your best choice, such as: jane@advocateforyou.com . Alternatively, you can use Gmail or any of the other generic email addresses like Yahoo or MSN/Live.

(A caveat – AOL is unreliable in delivering email to you. They seem to arbitrarily decide what newsletters they'll let you receive, for example. I explain this having been an AOL customer since 1993 and experiencing the loss of many things I expected to receive.)

Finally, a word about email and professionalism: This is best explained with an example. Suppose you need a lawyer to help you make out a will. You go online and identify three possible lawyers, so you send them each an email to inquire about their services. You receive replies from each, using the following email addresses:

>   psmith@lawyerforyou.com

>   psmith@hotmail.com

>   jeffysgrandma@aol.com

So which one strikes you as most professional?

As a health advocate who will be charged by your clients to handle health and finances, the two most personal aspects of any individual's life, you must look and behave professionally at all times – including in email.

K. How will you get around? What transportation will you need?

Who Can Help	Other Decisions This Will Affect	Cost Considerations	Priority
• Public transportation • Private services	• Your own transportation needs • Client services	Depend on your choices	Medium

Most business owners will need access to private transportation for any in-person work they do with clients. With the exception of very large cities, public transportation either takes too much time (don't forget – time is money) or isn't dependable enough to suffice for business.

If you don't already have a car or other vehicle to use to get around, be sure to choose one that is reliable, and keep it well maintained. You may also want to fund a membership in AAA or CAA another service to help you should you run into problems. (And don't forget – that will be a deductible expense.)

But transportation is mentioned here for another important reason. Many people who plan to go into private advocacy practice consider providing transportation to their clients, to doctor appointments, or for therapy or tests. It seems like a great service to provide, one which clients certainly need.

There are a handful of important reasons why you should not provide transportation to your clients, which we'll cover more thoroughly in Chapter Ten. But I mention that here because, as you decide what you'll use for transportation, know that you do not need to invest in something fancy and impressive for clients. Yes, they may see you park in their driveway one day, but no, they won't be riding alongside you in your car.

Discussions of cars and transportation takes us to our final business need, insurance.

L. What kinds of insurance will you need?

Who Can Help	Other Decisions This Will Affect	Cost Considerations	Priority
• Insurance brokers • Insurance websites	• Services you offer • Transportation • Contracts	Depend on your choices	Must be handled before you accept your first client.

Insurance – it's the one necessity nobody wants to think about or pay for. The goal is to make it so airtight that you never have to think about it again except when the bill comes due. Not easy.

In fact, it's a broad enough topic that it requires its own chapter, so we'll look at insurance more closely in Chapter Ten.

So many details!

But many of these business decisions only need to be made once, and if you've made them well, then you may never have to think about them again.

But then, many of them cost us money, too – money out of our pockets before we even take on our first client.

Sure! Go ahead!
This is a blank page, and it's
your book, so make some notes...

Chapter Seven
Money Matters: Expenses, Management and Funding

Have you recently won the lottery so that you have millions to spend and no fear of running out of money?

If not, then I'm afraid this chapter will be a reality cummupence. So far, most of our money mentions have been the mechanics of accepting payments – bringing money IN. After all, it seems so simple. "I'll tell people I'm going to advocate for them, and they'll pay me to do it!"

But, of course, it's not that simple. If it were, then anyone at all could hang out that shingle, say they were in business, then be wildly successful.

No. Going into business requires an enormous investment – in blood, sweat, tears and yes, cash. Without a real grasp on how that works, and solid planning in place, you'll be threatening your ability to start and grow a successful practice.

We'll assume here that you've already committed to the blood, sweat and tears. So now we'll delve into the exercise of figuring out how much money investment your new enterprise will require, especially early in the process.

Note: This chapter is intended to provide you with business start-up budgeting 101 – a new business owner's guide. It is not intended to substitute for the professional information provided to you by an accountant or CPA, or a lawyer.

A. Money Movement and Timing

When it comes to business, there are some basic money movement concepts to understand. If you hear business advisors using terms like "financials" or "budgets" – they are all referring to money movement – and are based on the following:

♦ What money will go out (expenses)

♦ What money will need to come in (income, also called revenue)

♦ The timing of when money comes in, compared to when it goes out (cash flow)

♦ What money is taxed vs what money is tax deductible

In this chapter we're going to deal with expenses, tax deductions and cash flow. Then we'll deal with income in Chapter Eight, in tandem with pricing your services.

Expenses

There are three main kinds of expenses: operating costs, capital costs and taxes.

Operating costs are those expenses you'll incur that won't contribute to any ongoing value in your business. Rent, utilities, office supplies, gas and oil to operate your car, business licenses, even payroll – these are simply the cost of running your business and don't show up in the real value of your business. You spend them, the money is gone, and they'll make no more contribution to what you achieve.

Capital costs or expenses are those that become a part of the value of your business. If you sold your business tomorrow, it would be priced by taking these assets into consideration. If you own a building, that's a capital expense. Any furniture owned by your company, or a car purchased in your company's name – those are capital expenses.

There are also some capital expenses you might not expect in this early stage. Your marketing may be considered a capital expense because it will contribute to your company's ongoing reputation – your brand.

Taxes

As a general rule, unless you have established a non-profit entity, when you make money, you'll need to pay taxes on it, and when you spend money on business-related expenses, you'll be able to deduct the amount from your taxes as a cost of doing business.

Surprisingly, it's really that easy, although with a few caveats.

First, you must be diligent about tracking and documenting every single penny you spend on your business, and every single penny you bring in as a result of your business activities.

Second, you must be careful not to assume something will be deductible when it won't be. For example, in the "old days" you could take anyone you ever knew to lunch, order wine and dessert, exchange business cards, and deduct it all. (You may remember hearing about "three martini lunches" in the 1950s and 60s.) But today there are very strict limits on the purchase of food and beverage as a business expense. Also, if you share the expense with your personal use of items such as your home, your car, your Internet use and others, then you can only deduct the percentage of use that was devoted to your business.

And third, don't use the "Hey, why not buy this, it's deductible!" excuse for something you WANT to purchase, as opposed to NEED to purchase. Buying a new computer because it's deductible doesn't mean you get it for free! It only means that if you spend $1000 on a new computer, and you are in the 25% tax bracket, then next year, when you file your taxes, Uncle Sam may give you a $250 break (although there are still other variables.)

Except to show you how to budget for taxes, I make no recommendations and provide no advice about business taxes. CPAs, accountants, bookkeepers – they are the people with tax expertise, and you should turn to them for guidance when it comes to your taxes.

Timing

There are three ways money is spent (or invested): expenses that occur only once, those that occur regularly (monthly, or annually) and those that only occur on irregular occasions. That means a good way to start budgeting for them is the same way.

Capital costs are either one-time, or irregular. Operating expenses recur on a regular basis, often monthly or quarterly.

Some expenses will shift over time. For example, one expense will be marketing, and your marketing expense will probably be higher in your first year than it will be in subsequent years. You know you'll see your CPA on a regular basis, but what your CPA charges you at tax time will probably be higher than what your CPA charges at other times during the year.

B. Budgeting and Tracking

Now that we better understand categories and timing, let's take a look at the actual expenses you'll have as you start your business. You've already gotten a good sense of what these will be in the last chapter. But here they are, listed for you, along with some considerations for deciding what to budget for each.

TASK #7

You'll find a starter budget process in the workbook that will allow you to begin developing your own expense budget. As you go through each line item, decide whether or not you'll need to budget for that item, and if you will, then take an educated guess as to what it will cost you for what period of time.

Budgeting Your Operating Expenses

Find a starter list of operating expenses for you to review with your accountant in the workbook. If you are unsure what a listed item refers to, you might find more information about it in Chapter Six.

Most of these expenses will be monthly, although you may choose to pay for some annually.

An important note about salaries and/or payments to subcontractors: Pay them first.

If you hire employees, you must pay them before you pay yourself or your other bills. If you hire freelancers – same thing – even though you won't be incurring freelancer expense with the same regularity.

Why is it so important to pay them first? Well, frankly, it's because they can talk! When we get to Chapter Nine – Marketing – you'll learn that the most important and influential form of marketing is word of mouth. It's the most powerful reason someone will hire you to be their advocate, and it's the most powerful deterrent, too. The minute you don't pay someone when or what they expect to be paid, you risk having them badmouth you. Thus – you must pay them first.

Budgeting Your Capital Expenses

Just as you've made an estimate of what you'll pay in operating expenses, you'll need to budget for capital expenses, too.

Your workbook contains a list of possible capital expenses. You may think of more. Make your best guestimates on what those expenses may be.

Setting Aside Money for Taxes

Here is a starter list of taxes for you to review with your accountant:

- ◆ Business Taxes will be incurred if you incorporate
- ◆ Income Taxes must be paid on profits
- ◆ Sales Taxes may be imposed by your locality or your state or province

And some aspects to taxes to be aware of – all of which will vary depending on what country you live in, or what your state or province requires.

Income taxes: Remember, since your income will be derived from clients paying you, you won't have an employer who withholds taxes from your income. In your first profit-making year, I promise you, you will be floored at your tax bill.

Unless you formed a corporation, you should also be aware that, by virtue of the fact that you are self-employed, you'll be paying almost twice as much into social security and Medicare (US) or CPP (Canada) as you did when you were someone else's employee. It makes sense, even if it seems expensive. If you are employed, you pay half and your employer pays half of your retirement to the government. But when you are self-employed, then you are both employer and employee – so you pay both portions.

It's wise to set aside the money you think you'll need for taxes as you earn it so you'll have what you need when the tax bill comes due. How much to set aside? A rule of thumb is to set aside the percentage you paid on last year's taxes. (If your income taxes totaled 25% of your income, then set aside 25% of what your clients pay you.) That should create a bit of a cushion, and if you don't need it all, it will be like found money once your tax bill has been paid.

Once you've paid income taxes for the first time after your business becomes profitable, you may also be required to pay quarterly taxes (your total income tax in the profitable year, divided by four, and paid the following year each quarter.)

Sales taxes are a whole 'nother animal. Most states and provinces do not tax services as a percentage of their price (at sale.) Most, if not all, do tax the sale of products. Check with your accountant to learn when you may be required to collect and remit sales taxes.

Tracking Your Money

Once you begin to spend and earn money for your business, you'll need to track it, compare it to your budget, make up any shortfalls that result, and celebrate your profits.

That tracking is simply comparing apples to apples: if you budget $12,000 for a year's worth of office rent, and you spent $12,800 then you'll need to adjust your budget to reflect that extra $800 worth of expense. If you make more or less money than you projected, then you'll need to accommodate for that, too. That comparison takes place through a method called "cash flow" – how the money flows in and out.

C. Cash Flow is King

I expect that this next step will produce somewhat of an "aha!" moment for you. It's going to help you tie together all the money pieces and see how they fit into your big picture.

Cash flow isn't a mystery. It's simply watching the timing of how money comes into your business as compared to how it goes out of your business.

Money flows in: As you invest money in yourself, as others invest money in your work, and as you produce income (revenue) from the work you do. (We'll talk about bringing in revenue in Chapter Eight.)

Money flows out: Through all the bills you pay, through the loans you repay (including to yourself), and through salaries or paychecks.

You have two goals for your cash flow: First, to have money flow in before it flows out, and second, for more to flow in than flows out.

Let's break it down in its simplest form by looking at two examples. These two cash flow statements are very simplistic, just to give you a sense of how they work. If your practice accounting will be very simple, then it may be all you need. If it will be more complex, then ask your accountant to help you develop a format that will serve your purposes. If, one day you decide to apply for a loan from a formal financial institution, their expectations will be much more complex than these examples.

Capitalization Can Make or Break Your Business

According to the US Small Business Administration, the number one reason businesses fail is because they are undercapitalized.

"Undercapitalized" simply means they ran out of money before they could really prove their business-worthiness. They didn't have enough capital (money) on hand before they got started. They wasted all their blood, sweat, tears and money – their entire investment – because they didn't get started with enough money.

Don't let that happen to you!

You've just spent time developing your budget in your Workbook. Take a look at that total you developed for Year 1.

That total is what you need, liquid and available, in order to capitalize your business, to ensure yourself that you won't have wasted your efforts and money to get started. It's not a guarantee that you'll be successful, of course. But it will, at least, give you a running start.

Why does all that money need to be liquid and available?

For many reasons, you may not be able to get at extra money if you begin to run out before your income ramps up from your business. For example, if you are currently employed, then your bank may let you take out a personal loan. But once you are self-employed in a brand new business, they may not be so willing to loan you money.

...And getting into credit card debt can be the kiss of business death.

CashFlow Statement #1:

This first cash flow statement assumes you are starting your practice with no money in the bank. Because you have no income yet, you're using a credit card to cover your expenses. Any amounts found in parentheses mean you are "in the hole" (less than $0).

	Starting Balance	$ that comes in from work with clients (revenue)	$ that goes out to pay bills, salaries and expenses	$ goes out to cover interest (only) on credit cards	Balance at the end of the month
Month 1:	$00	$00	(A)$7,000	$00	($7,000)
Month 2:	($7,000)	$500	$3,700	(B)$100	($10,300)
Month 3:	($10,300)	$1,500	$3,700	$200	($12,700)
Month 4:	($12,700)	$2,400	$3,700	$250	($14,250)
Month 5:	($14,250)	$1,600	(C)$4,200	$300	($17,150)
Month 6:	($17,150)	$2,100	$3,700	$375	($19,125)
Month 7:	($19,125)	$3,800	$3,700	$425	($19,450)
Month 8:	($19,450)	(D)$1,400	$3,700	$450	($21,300)
Month 9:	($21,300)	$3,000	(C)$5,000	$525	($23,825)
Month 10:	($23,825)	$3,400	$3,700	$600	($24,725)
Month 11:	($24,725)	$4,200	$3,700	$650	($24,875)
Month 12:	($24,875)	$5,700	$3,700	$700	($22,925)
Month 13:	($22,925)	$6,200	$3,700	$550	($20,975)

A = as you get started, you will have legal costs, insurance, marketing costs and more.

B = You'll begin paying interest on credit cards. These are just guesstimates and depend on the interest rate for the card you use.

C = some months your expenses will be a bit higher – maybe you add more to your website, or you attend a conference in another state.

D = one month you'll take an income hit – end of the year holidays, or maybe you get sick.

As you can see from Cashflow Statement #1, after 13 months you will end up almost $21,000 in debt with thousands of dollars in credit card interest still left to repay. Not only will you be solidly in the red, your stress level, and frustration at credit card bills, will be over the top. You will very likely go out of business, even though you'll still be responsible for repaying that $21,000.

Out of business after one year? Yes. Because you were undercapitalized. You jumped into business without setting aside any money to keep it afloat before you began bringing in enough income.

Cashflow Statement #2

In your Workbook, you developed a budget alongside a sample budget I developed to provide an example. In that sample budget, we estimated it would cost $27,000 to pay for your first year in business.

So for the second cash flow statement (at right), we'll capitalize the business with that $27,000 so we can see what the differences are. In this case there will be no credit card expense because we don't go into the hole each time we put something on credit. There will be loans to pay back though, either to ourselves or to the people who loaned us money. When agreements with investors are made ahead of time the payback terms can be negotiated so the money doesn't get paid back immediately.

In the second cash flow statement, you actually end up with $2,600 extra at the end of 13 months. You may still have loans to repay, but if so, you'll repay them out of revenue you are bringing in. Assuming you borrowed that initial $27,000, you will have already paid it down by almost a third. No frustration over credit card debt, and no sleepless nights from being in the red.

And best of all, you'll still be in business.

TASK #8

Develop your own cashflow statement using your
projected first year budget.
Make both sets of assumptions, capitalized vs uncapitalized,
then decide which way you want to start your business.

Now that you have both your budget and your cash flow projections, about once a month, reconcile your expenditures against your budget to see where you stand.

If you find you're bringing in revenue faster than anticipated, well, then, halleluyah!

But if not, you'll need to figure out how to fill in the gaps. As long as you are capitalized, you'll have some money accessible to carry you through any of those months you may be in the red.

Cashflow Statement #2

	Starting Balance (Capital Invested)	$ that comes in from work with clients (revenue)	$ that goes out to pay bills, salaries and expenses	$ goes out to cover loan payments, including interest	Balance at the end of the month
Month 1:	$27,000	$00	(A)$7,000	$00	$20,000
Month 2:	$20,000	$500	$3,700	$00	$16,800
Month 3:	$16,800	$1,500	$3,700	$00	$14,600
Month 4:	$14,600	$2,400	$3,700	$00	$13,300
Month 5:	$13,300	$1,600	(C)$4,200	$00	$10,700
Month 6:	$10,700	$2,100	$3,700	$00	$9,100
Month 7:	$9,100	$3,800	$3,700	(B)$1,000	$8,200
Month 8:	$8,200	(C)$1,400	$3,700	$1,000	$4,900
Month 9:	$4,900	$3,000	(D)$5,000	$1,000	$1,900
Month 10:	$1,900	$3,400	$3,700	$1,000	$600
Month 11:	$600	$4,200	$3,700	$1,000	$100
Month 12:	$100	$5,700	$3,700	$1,000	$1,100
Month 13:	$1,100	$6,200	$3,700	$1,000	$2,600

A = as you get started, you will have legal costs, insurance, marketing costs and more.

B = at six months you begin paying back the loans you started your business with (maybe to yourself, or maybe to others). This amount pays back part of the principle owed, plus the interest.

C = one month you'll take a hit – end of the year holidays, or maybe you get sick.

D = some months your expenses will be a bit higher – maybe you add more to your website, or you attend a conference in another state.

If you're looking for a way to automate this process, you might invest in one of the software programs available for business financials. Quicken, Quickbooks, Freshbooks and others help you stay organized, do the "math", highlight potential problems or mistakes, and at the end of the year, provide a download to the tax software your accountant (or you) will use.

If you do choose to use a software program, it's best to ask your accountant which one will interface with his or her system to make it all work seamlessly.

D. What Will It (Really) Cost to Start Your Business?

I'm often asked that question: how much do I need to start a private advocacy practice? But the answer is complex. There is no one-size-fits-all number.

There are many variables that can't be accommodated for by providing a simple number. But I can provide a more solid answer to those who read this book, because you'll find the support for the answer here, and you'll be able to understand where the numbers come from.

Spending? Or Investing?

The maxim is true – you do need to spend some money to make some money. You cannot go into business, manage it professionally, grow it, and profit from it (even if you establish a non-profit) if you don't spend some money at the beginning.

But there may be a better concept to use than the idea of "spending." I prefer to think of starting a business as an investment. The money you put into a business at the outset, and then ongoing as it serves to grow and strengthen your business, is an investment in your future.

In effect, by spending that money to get your business started, you're saying "I'm more confident in my ability to start and grow this business than I am in any other way to grow my money!"

Honestly, if you can't buy that, then going into business may not be the right thing for you anyway.

So here it is: Just as we discovered during the budgeting process in your workbook, I estimate that doing a good job of establishing your business, and to avoid undercapitalization, will require between $25,000 and $30,000 depending on which services you will provide and where you live.

That $25,000 assumes you work from home (no rent), that you spend a minimum on new equipment, and that you borrow at least part of the total and therefore have some interest payments that must be made in that first year. (You can find the actual estimates I've used in the budget in the Workbook.)

Why do services matter? Your services define delivery. For example, an advocate who spends more time on the road meeting with clients, or attending appointments, will also spend more money in gas, and will have fewer billable hours (although those fewer billable hours become part of the cash flow, but not part of a start-up expense budget.)

Why does geography matter? Because the cost of living varies – and along with the cost of living, business expenses will be higher, too.

The important part of these numbers is to understand that they are the amount that will be needed to start because, even though you'll have many start-up expenses that need to be paid, you won't have any money coming in for a while. Don't forget, too, that these expenses are in addition to your living expenses. They don't account for putting food on your table or clothes on your back, or even providing your own health insurance. They are business-only expenses.

E. Where Will All that Money Come From?

To most potential-business-owners, the only surprise that is bigger than the $25,000 to $30,000 start-up figures is the answer to the question of where that money must come from.

That answer is: You'll have to scrape it together on your own.

Traditional lenders will not lend money to start ups because the risk of not being paid back is just too high. So many new businesses fail, and they can't afford to be caught supporting a failing business; the law and their shareholders won't let them. You may KNOW you'll be the ONE person who will NEVER FAIL, but on paper you look just like everyone else. Very few, if any, lending institutions will lend you money in your start-up phase.

I'm often asked about "small business loans" like SBA loans. But those loans aren't intended for start-ups. They are supplied to businesses that already have a track record, and are looking to expand their businesses, or are creating new revenue streams.

Non-profits can apply for grants, but when a newly started non-profit is compared to one that's been in business for a while and has a track record for raising funds on its own, the newbie will fall short.

With very few exceptions (the truth being, I don't even know what those exceptions are), you'll have to raise your start-up money yourself. Your own savings, a second mortgage, your Great Aunt Genevieve, a generous neighbor, or any combination thereof – these individuals may invest in you.

You may have some personal resources you can tap into: a line of credit at your bank, or a second mortgage on your home. You may have an old life insurance policy that allows for borrowing.

Retirement savings? Not so fast. That's an important question for your financial advisor or accountant. Retirement savings is a sacred cow, but for a select few, depending on circumstances, it may be a viable option.

Individuals who invest in you are called "angel investors." You might invest half the money yourself, then ask others to share the remaining 50%. If you do borrow from others, whether they are family or friends or anyone else, then be sure to put a written agreement into place, offering a fair, market-appropriate amount of interest, with specific payment terms, which both parties sign. Ask your lawyer to help you draw up such an agreement.

And don't forget – any money you borrow needs to be repaid. Even if you are repaying your own savings account, build it into your budget so that you won't be paying taxes on money you "loaned" to yourself.

We've done a yeoman's job of covering all those nightmares – er – I mean, financial expenses small businesses are concerned with... from capitalization to cash flow...

Now let's take a look at the positive, more pleasant side of the financial life of a practice...

Let's talk about income!

Estimates Are Guesstimates

One of the aspects of starting a business that is often overwhelming to new entrepreneurs is that they don't understand that the entire planning process is one big GUESS. Seriously. Any sort of projection you make, whether it's about the number of clients you might have, or the amount you will need to spend on gas for your car, will be a guess. An educated one, perhaps. But a guess all the same.

But that's OK! I promise you that Bill Gates only guesstimated, as did Ben and Jerry. Lou Z. Bissness guesstimated, too, when he founded Lou's Handholders International. (What – you've never heard of Lou Z. Bissness? Well, that's because he wasn't a very good guesstimator.)

Your goal with guesstimating is to always lean conservative. If you are estimating income – then figure you'll make a little less than you expect. If you are estimating expenses, then you can be quite sure they'll be more than you expect. So guess accordingly.

You'll be more accurate than you expect if you guesstimate expenses following these recommendations:

Make your initial guess an educated one based on research or background knowledge.

Multiply it – by at least 120%, up to 200%. If you think an item will cost $100, it will more likely cost $120 to $200. So budget for that more conservative, higher amount.

Be flexible. Be willing to guess again, more accurately, as you learn more about that specific expense. You'll get better at it each month as you reconcile your budget.

Chapter Eight
Money Matters: Revenue, Profits and Pricing Your Services

Hopefully you've recovered from the Chapter Seven reality check of the cost of starting and running your business.

It's far more fun to discuss how you'll bring money into your business, and so, in hopes of supporting your recovery, that's what we'll tackle here.

One of the questions I'm asked most frequently is, "How much money do private health advocates make?" As you can already see based on the expenses exercise we've just done, the answer is a definite, "It depends!" There are a dozen variables ranging from what services you provide, to where you live, to what you charge.

Even more frequently than asking about total income, potential advocates ask me, "How much should I charge?"

Both are good questions. Let's figure out the answers.

The Income Side of the Equation

Assuming one of your business goals will be to bring in more money than you spend in your business, that making a profit is a goal (or at least breaking even if you run a non-profit) we need to focus on making sure the amount of money you bring in to your business will meet your goals. And further, that the money you bring in will be what you have earned, not borrowed from somewhere else.

In order to know whether the money you earn will create a profit for you, we need to know how much it costs to be in business – which is what we figured out in Chapter Seven. As we move forward in this chapter with figuring out the many aspects of income, we'll use the example expenses total from your Workbook = $27,000 for your first year.

So we have laid the groundwork for developing our pricing. We want to be sure we price our work so that it yields enough to cover all our expenses – and more.

How Much Profit Do You Want to Make?

I realize that seems like a silly question; most of us would answer, "as much as I can!"

That's a fair answer, of course, but it makes accountants roll over in their graves, and makes it impossible to do our business planning.

So just like we guesstimated our expenses, we're going to guesstimate a fair amount of income and profit, and we're going to base that on what we would want our salary to be. In the first years of doing business, that's a fair goal – that any money over and above your other business expenses will be your salary.

All examples here will be for a one-person business. If you develop a partnership, or there is more than one person, then do this same math for all the people involved.

For example: say you decide your profit/salary should be $50,000 (a fair salary for one person starting out) – then you'll need to add that $50,000 to your other expenses. That means, in our example, that you'll need to bring in $77,000 in Year 1. ($27,000 worth of expenses plus $50,000.)

You might consider, too, estimating a high end and a low end. Your low end might be that $50,000 / $77,000 and maybe for a high end you want to make $100,000 in your first year. In that case you'll need to bring in $127,000.

Projected Profit / Salary	Plus Expenses	Business Income / Revenue Needed
$50,000 (low end)	+ $27,000	= $77,000
$100,000 (high end)	+ $27,000	= $127,000

A note about profits and salaries:

I am taking some liberties in my examples, because every person's situation will be different, and because salary or profit in one location will be regarded very differently from the way it's regarded somewhere else.

It's important to note that a self-employed "salary" cannot be fairly compared to the salary you receive from an employer. An employer salary is usually accompanied by benefits, like health insurance, and that is not considered in our list of expenses, nor is it included in the 'salary' we've described here.

Income as a self-employed person is affected positively by some factors, making it seem like more than it really sounds, and affected negatively by others, making it worth less than it seems.

On the positive side: Working for yourself, in particular from home, means you have many benefits that aren't accounted for in an employer salary, such as flexibility, the fact that you don't need a work wardrobe, lunches can be pulled out of the refrigerator, and your commute may be far less expensive and stressful, and others.

On the negative side: Your money won't come in on a regular basis (another reason to be well-capitalized before you start). Also, since you'll be self-employed, any profit you make that is taken as salary will be taxed differently than if you made that money through an employer.

But again – on the positive side – that's why you'll have an accountant to help you figure all this out. And there are ways of accounting for your income – whether you call it profit or salary – that will make it taxed more favorably, or make your benefits improve deductibility. For these reasons, if for no others, your accountant will be worth his or her weight in gold.

Figuring Out How Much to Charge

So now that we know how much we need to bring in, how do we do that?

Here are several approaches to figuring out how much to charge for the work you do. Each of them will allow you to look at your pricing from a different angle. Ultimately, what you charge for your services should reflect your answers to all of these approaches.

In this section we're going to work toward developing an hourly rate. You may or may not ever really charge and bill this exact rate, but an hourly rate is a great place to start.

Here is the list of approaches for developing your pricing, with explanations forthcoming.

1. Billable Hours
2. The Concept of Value
3. Assessing Your Competition
4. Starting – Somewhere!

1. Billable Hours

While it doesn't really matter what we call it, most of the work we do as health advocates would be categorized as consulting work. As health advocates, we don't have history to draw from to figure out how to price our services. But we can find some history and data about consultants to help us.

The important statistic we want to use is the one that tells us that consultants typically spend 58 to 62 percent of their time actually working with their clients.[12] The rest of the time is spent on administrative tasks (from filing and bookkeeping to returning phone calls), or unbillable work. (More about billable hours later in this chapter.)

For new consultancies, the amount of time will be even less, at least in the first year. That's because, during the first year, far more time must be devoted to marketing and acquiring new clients, also called "sales." So for our business-start-up purposes, we're going to lower that number to 50 percent of a 40-hour work week.

That means that in the beginning, in any given week, you will be paid, on average, for only about 20 hours of work. You may be able to expand the number of hours by working more than a 40 hour week (In fact, I can guarantee that early in your new practice, you'll work far more than 40 hours per week, if only on marketing.) But remember, we want to figure on the conservative side.

Over a year's time, that average 20 hours/week will also be affected by everything from vacation, to holidays, to when your car breaks down on the highway, or the school calls because your child is sick, to anything else. So our 20 hours per week will probably translate, conservatively, to only about 950 hours in a year.

With those numbers, we can craft our first approach to figuring out how much to charge for our services. We are going to divide our expenses plus profit for the first year by the number of hours we can bill for. We can do that for the high end and the low end of our profitability structure.

Business Income / Revenue Needed	Divided by the number of billable hours	What we need to charge, on average, per hour.
Low End = $77,000	÷ 950 hours	$81.05
High End = $127,000	÷ 950 hours	$133.68

So, based on billable hours alone, we know we will need to charge between $81 and $134 per hour to stay in business and pay ourselves between $50,000 and $100,000 in our first year.

---

12 From Kennedy Information Research: www.KennedyInfo.com

2. The Concept of Value (Compared to Alternative Consequences)

You may be looking at that range of $81 to $134 per hour wondering whether anyone would ever pay you that amount of money.

The answer is both simple and complex. They certainly will - as long as they see the value of what you bring to them.

The first aspect of value to consider is the comparison to any given patient's (or caregiver's) alternative consequences. Alternative consequences are all the things that can happen, usually negative, if someone decides not to hire you and pay you, no matter how much you charge. Alternatives for some patients might be that they will get sicker or die. Others will remain fearful. Still others, like caregivers, won't find the relief they need. And still others will go bankrupt with no one to help them get claims paid or hospital bills reduced.

The value of considering alternative consequences comes into play no matter how much you charge, and like other value propositions, can be used in your marketing. The translation to marketing is focusing on benefits. The main benefit of what you offer, at the price you offer it, is that you will make the alternative consequences disappear or at least be diminished. We'll look at this more closely in Chapter Nine.

The other aspect of value may come as a surprise to you. That is, the more you charge, the more likely you are to acquire a client. I know that seems backward, because for most purchases we ever make, it's a lower price we are drawn to. But when it comes to products or services we think have more value, we will pay more.

Two examples:

First, think of golf shirts. You can buy a plain white golf-type shirt from Walmart for $11.99. Or you can buy one from a high-end retailer with a little polo horse, or an alligator on it for $39.95. No matter which one you buy, it's going to go with every skirt or pair of shorts you own, and will cover the top of you.

Now you know perfectly well that some people will pay that higher price for what seems to many others to be the exact same thing.

Why will some people pay more? Because they value that little logo on the shirt. That's the same reason they buy Lexus, Hartmann and Minalo Blahnik. Granted, in some cases there is more quality or extra built-in functions, but in all cases, no matter the price or logo on a car, a suitcase, or pair of shoes, it will get you from point A to point B.

The value in all these cases is in the brand. Over the years, those brands have developed their reputations of being higher quality (maybe) and higher price (always) and when you wear a shirt with an alligator or drive a Lexus, then those brands speak volumes about you. They say you can afford them. And that idea of being able to afford more expensive brands is very appealing to some people.

So how do we apply that to a health advocacy practice? By building our brands based on quality and value, and by providing quality and value to build our brands. They go hand-in-hand. Included in the high-quality brand is high-end pricing which will ideally sound very expensive at first, until someone realizes the benefit of paying that much money – avoiding the alternative consequences.

Example Two:

Years ago, we had a Cocker Spaniel named Zeke. Zeke got loose one day, and about nine weeks later, the Schnauzer across the street gave birth to six little "Schnockers." They were just adorable – but neither the neighbor, Ann Marie, nor our family, wanted to add a new dog to our families. So Ann Marie put an ad in the newspaper, "Puppies - free to a good home!," and waited for the phone to ring.

The phone never rang. Not once.

We realized that by giving the puppies away for free, they had no perceived value. If we thought they were worthless, then the people who saw the ad did, too. So Ann Marie put a new ad in the paper, "Schnocker Puppies: $50" – and her phone rang off the hook.

Selling Schnockers had nothing to do with branding. No one could compare them to the pricing of other Schnockers, and certainly, there isn't much esteem in being able to say you own what amounts to a mutt! No – the only reason Ann Marie could sell all the puppies was because she assigned a high price to them – which gave them value.

The lesson for health advocates, Schnockers and alligators notwithstanding, is – don't be afraid to charge higher prices! To a point (and no, I don't know what that point might be), your services will have value because you have charged high prices for them.

3. Assessing your competition

What does your competition charge?

That question assumes you actually have competition, and for most areas of the United States and Canada, as of 2012, you may not have much local competition to compare to.

But not all competition is local, nor will all competition be readily identifiable. For example, if you are a billing or claims advocate, your competition could be located anywhere in the United States. Those are services that don't require you to meet in someone's living room.

Further, more and more services are being delivered by telecommunications of some sort, including the Internet and shared patient forums. A diagnosis research advocate might be replaced by WebMD. A mental health advocate might be able to deliver services by computer camera via sites like Skype or Google Hangouts from anywhere in the world.

You'll want to do a thorough job of finding out what alternatives there are to your individual services, then balance your pricing accordingly.

4. Starting – Somewhere!

Based on the first three pricing approaches, you should have narrowed down what you want to charge by the hour to deliver the value you want to deliver, and bring in the revenue you need to cover your expenses and your profit / salary.

You're probably left with a range, as in "Oh, maybe I should charge $100 or maybe $125 an hour."

How do you decide that final number?

I'm suggest you go for the higher number – and add a little. If that's your range, then you should decide instead to charge $135 or even $150 an hour.

Why? A few reasons.

First, because you can always lower the number, but you'll be hard pressed to raise it. Picture yourself telling a client you've decided to begin charging him more. Now picture yourself telling a client you've decided to charge him a little less. Which one will make your client happier?

Second, because in the next section of this chapter we're going to fool around with the pricing a little, developing formats and packaging which will actually reduce your hourly charge. So, you want to start high so that when you lower it, it will be where it needs to be.

Third, because you're worth it. Yes, you really are.

How will you know your pricing is right?

Thirty-five years ago, when I started my first business, this piece of wisdom was shared with me by a mentor I had at the time. It has stuck with me, and has been shared with dozens of entrepreneurs ever since. That is: You'll know you're charging the right amount when you feel like you are obscenely expensive to hire, but you have more business than you can handle.

I've been there – and it does feel good, and right. You'll get there, too.

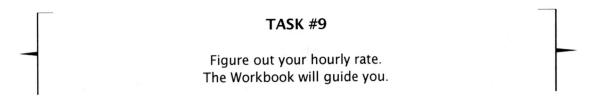

TASK #9

Figure out your hourly rate.
The Workbook will guide you.

The Holy Grail – Billable Hours

A few notes regarding billable hours, before we begin the discussion of how you will actually charge for your services...

A billable hour is exactly what it sounds like – an hour spent doing your advocacy work for a client; an hour for which you will be paid for the expertise you bring to the relationship.

How Much Do Other Advocates Charge?

Unless the "other advocates" you are asking about are your direct competitors, then what they charge is mostly irrelevant.

That said, it does make sense for you to understand the range of charges, as long as you understand that your charges should be somewhere in the middle, and should be influenced by those factors we discuss here (services, skill level, location, etc.)

In the United States (and translatable to Canadian dollars, too) some advocates charge as little as $40 an hour, which I believe is too low and was being charged by someone who didn't have the benefit of the exercises in this book.

The most I've heard one advocate charged is $350/hour, but he had clients all over the world and more than a decade of excellent reputation on which to base his pricing.

Contrast that with a non-billable hour which is an hour of work you won't be paid for, such as driving or bookkeeping or arguing with the phone company.

Your goal, as a business owner, is to devote as many hours as possible in your workday to billable hours, and to keep your non-billable hours to a minimum.

Not that non-billable hours are always a waste of time – they aren't. If you put your hours to good use like using them for marketing tasks, or saving money on the purchase of a new client tracking software package, or if you go to a conference where you learn about the many ways you can recruit new clients or how to navigate an insurance claim – there's little wasted time there. But those tasks will subtract a chunk of your billable hours.

When you first get started, you'll find yourself spending too many hours that aren't billable – so try to balance those hours by making them useful even if they aren't billable.

As your practice matures, and you have a track record with plenty of satisfied clients telling their friends good things about you, you'll find yourself increasing your number of billable hours each year.

Of course, there are a limited number of billable hours available in any given period of time. We have based our hourly rate on 40 hours of work in a week. But some of you will actually work 50 or 60 or 70 hours. Does that mean you'll make more money because more of those hours will be billable? Possibly. But you'll read later in this chapter about efficiency and estimating time – two important keys to getting paid for billable hours.

That limit to the number of billable hours also frames the number of clients you can juggle at any one time. Figure out an average number of hours you want to work in a week, or month, then be sure you don't contract to do any more work than that. If you are already running full load with 45 hours of committed time this week, don't sign a contract with someone who will need an additional 10 hours immediately. Overload means mistakes, and mistakes can sink your practice ship. Either try to put off the new potential client until next week, or month, or look at bringing in a subcontractor to help out.

There are ways to increase your number of billable hours and therefore, your income. As time goes on, efficiency will play a role in increasing your billable hours. You might also look at hiring someone, including freelancers, to begin attending to some of the administrative or marketing tasks you do, paying them less than your hourly rate, but increasing your number of work hours so you can pay them, too. If it takes an hour to answer emails that someone else can answer, then hiring someone like a virtual assistant to handle them at $35 an hour is a bargain when you can charge $135 for that same hour.

Your Hourly Rate is a Target

Now that we have an hourly rate, I'm going to tell you that you probably won't ever really make that hourly rate. More likely you'll make less, sometimes much less. Rarely will you make more. Think of your new hourly rate as a target that you work around, or perhaps more to the point, that you subtract from.

There are several reasons you won't make that amount of money for that amount of time. Sometimes your pricing will fluctuate based on the psychology of working with clients and potential clients. Other times it will be because you haven't allotted enough time for a project. Or sometimes you may have allotted too much time, but you worked so efficiently that your client will be paying you for time you didn't really need.

Avoiding the Great Pricing Abyss

Scenario: You're getting ready to start your new business, and you identify a potential lawyer to work with. So you call the lawyer and ask her how much she will charge you to help you set up your business. She replies that she isn't sure, but that her hourly rate is $200 an hour. Do you hire her?

Probably not. Why? Because that $200 doesn't tell you anything. You don't know what the deliverables will be. You have no idea how long it will take her to do the work. You may be able to compare that $200 an hour to another lawyer's $250 per hour – but without knowing anything else about her ability to do the work, there is really no comparison to be made. It might take Lawyer A 10 hours to do the work, but Lawyer B might complete it in 7.5 hours, meaning she would actually cost you less.

That's how potential clients will feel if you give them an hourly rate and hope they will hire you. Your hourly rate doesn't really tell them anything and leaves them feeling as if they are opting in to something that may cost them thousands and thousands of dollars – money they may not have. They can't grasp the size of that abyss.

So the first piece of advice is to never give out your hourly rate as an isolated piece of information. You need to supply an endpoint, or at least a fairly accurate estimate of the total so they can know what will be coming from their pockets and for what amount of work. Yes, you may have to add on to the amount later, after some discussion. But you need a defined endpoint as your place to start.

The Psychology of Pricing

Sometimes pricing has less to do with actual numbers and more to do with the perception of the person who will pay that amount.

We've already discussed one aspect of the psychology of pricing; that is, that people will ascribe a higher value to something they pay a lot of money for – like alligators, polo ponies or Schnockers.

But there is also the very human desire to feel as if we are getting a good deal. Retailers, in particular, use this sort of pricing to encourage people to buy from them. "SALE!" makes people run in to a store to buy something, even though the price may be exactly the same as it always is. My favorite is the "Buy One, Get One Free" – when we fail to pay attention to the fact that they just doubled the price for the first one. Yet, people still buy extras.

We can use some of this psychology, too, to help our potential clients make the decision to hire us, and to help them feel as if they are getting a good deal. We do that by creating packages or products that ensure we'll get the amount we need for our work, but help them feel as if they won't be paying through the nose for our services.

The easiest way to understand this is by examples. These are real world examples being used today by health advocates. You can use them, too – all of them, or just a few of them.

A Dozen "Bargains": How to Charge for Your Services

Idea #1: Client Assessments or Situation Analysis

The first problem in the previous scenario is that no scope of work was defined. The scope of work is the list of activities or deliverables that you and your potential client have developed and agreed upon as what you will do for the amount of money that person will pay you.

So that's where you'll want to start – by working with the client to develop your scope of work. You'll do that by figuring out what he needs, figuring out how long it will take and what resources will be needed to make it happen, then pricing your services based on that scope of work.

Too many advocates do assessments for free, performing long interviews, drawing up pages of paperwork descriptions and agreements. Then, unless they already have an agreement in place with the client, they don't get hired to do the work after all. Very frustrating, a waste of time, and use of time that might have been put toward billable hours.

Instead, I suggest a different approach; that is, to charge a fair amount for developing the assessment (the scope of work) – so that you are being paid right at the get-go for your expertise.

But here's where the human wish to feel like he's getting a good deal comes in: Tell the potential client that you are going to charge him for developing the needs assessment (or scope of work, or list of deliverables – they are all names for the same thing) – then tell him that if he hires you at the end, you will subtract that amount (or part of the amount) from the total cost of the work.

> *"Mr. Jones. I see that your situation is quite complex. I can't give you even a ball park price for helping you unless we agree on the scope of work. I want to be sure you and I both have the same expectations for the services I'll perform for you. I suggest we work together on developing an assessment of your situation and needs. I charge $249 for that assessment. When it's finished, we have a very clear list of services and outcomes, and I'll be able to give you a definitive price for doing the work. Then, if you agree to the price of the project, I'll subtract that $249 fee I charged you for the assessment from your final invoice."*

There's an endpoint for Mr. Jones. It may be the first of many endpoints, but he knows what the initial work will cost him, and knows what you'll deliver for that amount of money. Part of your agreement should be to hand over the report to him when you're finished with it so he feels as if he has paid for something tangible.

(Re: the $249. You can charge that, or more, or less. When you first begin doing assessments, it will take you longer, and later, when you get more efficient, they won't take as long. Remember, the idea is to cover your hourly rate as you develop the assessment.)

Idea #2: Project Rates

When you do an assessment such as the one you did for Mr. Jones, you'll end up knowing about how long it will take to do the work for him. So, when you report back to Mr. Jones, you can quote him a project rate that reflects a discount.

> *"Mr. Jones, in order to perform this list of tasks and create this list of outcomes, I estimate it will take me 15 hours of time. But I offer reduced pricing for any project that takes more than 12 hours. I usually charge $150 an hour, but I will complete this scope of work, even if it takes me more than 15 hours, for $2175."* (Math: $150 x 12 hours plus $125 x 3 hours = $2175).

Now Mr. Jones feels like you are giving him a good deal, and your effective hourly rate (EHR) comes out to $145 (assuming you've estimated the work well - see the Sidebar in Chapter Twelve).

A word of caution here: If you did tell Mr. Jones you would subtract the fee for doing the assessment, then don't forget to add into the scope of work the time it already took you to do that assessment. If you estimate the scope of work will take you 15 hours to perform, and it takes you two hours to develop the assessment, then your actual estimate for time for the scope needs to be 17 hours – and that's the number you give to Mr. Jones. The numbers above will shift for this alternative, but remember, you're not into volunteering your time. You're trying to build a business and be paid fairly.

Are Advocacy Services Insurance Reimbursable?

Potential clients often ask their new advocates whether insurance will pay for the advocate's services. So far as I know, the answer is no. No health insurer I know of is reimbursing for a private advocate's services.

If you're just starting out as an advocate, you may be thinking that it would be great to get a client's insurer to pay you! That way you wouldn't have to have the conversation about money, and you could keep working for them until the insurance money ran out.....

But it doesn't work that way. And frankly, I don't think you want it to, for a number of reasons.

First, because the minute the insurer is committed to paying, the insurer gets to tell you what to do – based on what they will reimburse for. If they say "no," then what will you do? One of the biggest reasons a client hires a private advocate to begin with is because they feel like their insurer and doctors aren't providing what they need. If you are beholden to the insurer then you'll be in that same boat.

Second, because you'll end up being a paperwork pusher and not an advocate. Doctors tell us that one-third to one-half their staff are devoted to billing insurance and Medicare. Do you want to spend all your time billing? It's not billable time – it's your time.

Third, even if you were reimbursed, even if you were willing to do all that billing, you would wait and wait and wait for payment. Insurers often wait 90 to 120 days to pay, so the work you do and bill by mid-January doesn't get paid to you until May. Medicare is even worse, often making doctors and hospitals wait up to 180 days for payment. That means you'd be lucky to see a check in July for the work you did in January.

And fourth, instead of you charging an hourly rate or a project rate, you will be told how much money you are going to get. You think your services are worth $150 per hour? Think again. A reimbursement will look more like $50 or $75. That might not sound too bad, except that for every hour you worked, you spent another 20 minutes to half hour putting together the bills for reimbursement – so it really boils down to more like $35 or $60 per hour.

For these reasons and more I suggest you fuggedabout insurance reimbursements for your private advocacy work. It's just not worth it.

Idea #3: Body of Hours

For some clients, your work will be ongoing and too difficult to estimate. This would be the case when you are hired by an adult child who lives out of state, but your actual patient-client will be Mom who lives near you. The adult child may just want to hire you for tasks as they pop up, such as stepping in if Mom is suddenly hospitalized, or to review her medical bills once a month where it might take five hours in July but twelve hours in August.

In this case you can do much like you did for the project rate. Tell the adult child that you can supply a body of hours for a fixed price that is less than your hourly rate would be.

> *"Mr. Loman, I would love to be on call to help with your mother's care. I suggest you purchase a body of hours of my time. I'll track that time against the services I perform, and will issue you a report once a week (or month or with each interface) so you know how the time has been spent. Once we're down to the last few hours, we can do the same thing again. I typically charge $150 per hour, but we could write an agreement for 20 hours for $2,500. Does that work for you?"*

Once again, Mr. Loman will feel as if he's getting a good deal, and in effect, you will have agreed to an EHR of $125 per hour for 20 hours of work.

If you do decide to take this route, try to make that body of hours big enough so that you won't be constantly returning to Mr. Loman for money. That eats up time – time that could be used instead for billable hours. You might also consider starting with a smaller body of hours, then for the next go-round, increasing to many more hours, depending on how well you, Mr. Loman and his mother are working together.

Idea #4: Monthly Retainers

Another approach similar to the project rate is to develop a monthly retainer agreement with your client. This works very well for a scenario such as your work with Mr. Loman and his mother, and helps the paying client feel as if he or she has control over costs.

Develop a list of services and tasks you'll perform each month, and assign a number of hours to them. Then write a contract that allows for that number of hours, on average, per month, over a six or 12 month period. You'll bill the client for that same number of hours each month, and you'll track your time. Some months you may not use the entire body of hours, and other months you may use more, but the client still writes the same amount check each month.

> *Mrs. Anderson – this list of services can probably be accomplished in an average of 12 hours each month. I usually charge $150 per hour, but if you'd like me to work on a retainer with you, I'll bill you for only 10 hours each month, but will provide those 12 hours of service. If the work requires 15 hours one month, then I'll work only 9 hours the next month. If the work requires only 10 hours one month, I can*

do a few extra hours the next. But bottom line, you'll pay me $1500 per month, and I'll track my time against our 12 hours per month retainer.

Be sure you document all the time you spend, and provide reports to Mrs. Anderson on a regular basis. As you close in on the end of the retainer agreement, do a final reconciliation, then either work off any remaining hours, or invoice Mrs. Anderson for the extra hours you spent.

Of course, it's entirely possible Mrs. Anderson will simply want to re-up on your retainer, too. She's gotten used to your help and appreciates all your assistance.

Idea #5: Monthly Memberships or Subscriptions

A variation on the monthly retainer is a monthly membership. You may reach a point where you have developed some value-added services, like an informative newsletter, or online courses, or a series of videos, "do-it-yourself" empowerment lessons. At the point you are adding to your repertoire of teaching/learning products that would be worth a subscription -type pricing, you can begin to charge a monthly membership fee for access to all those products, even access to you, too.

This is definitely something you would handle through your website. The monthly subscription fee will be dependent on what the package offers access to. A combination of your newsletter, a monthly video, and 30 minutes of your time might be worth $59 per month, for example. Not all your clients would ever take advantage of their 30 minutes. (And some clients will push their 30 minutes into an hour.) These subscriptions could be automatically billed meaning, once they are set up, you have no more administrative time involved except for delivering whatever your monthly promise is.

They can be quite lucrative (100 people x $59/ month is $5,900!) but beware that you don't over extend your promised time. If all 100 people use their 30 minutes and no more, that's 50 hours of time at an average of $118 per hour – less than your one-on-one time at your planned for billable hourly rate of $125+ (or whatever your rate is.)

Idea #6: Daily Rates

Some advocate services, such as sitting by a hospital bedside, require more than just an hourly or project rate. You won't ever know how long someone will be in the hospital, or how long it will take to sit by their side at a half-dozen doctor or lab appointments.

In cases like this you might want to charge a daily rate instead which promises them eight hours at a little less than your hourly rate for those eight hours.

Idea #7: Percentage of Savings

Those who work in insurance billing or medical bill reduction have been known to charge a percentage of what they save the client. This sounds like a grand idea on paper – if you save a client $35,000 and your agreement is to keep 25% of the savings, that $8,750 is a nice chunk of change!

But there is danger in this approach, and if you've been doing this kind of work, on these terms, for any length of time, you know exactly what it is. The chances that someone has $8,750 in a checking account ready to hand off to you, are slim to none. Even though you've saved them part of the bill, you have really just saved them something they didn't really have to spend to begin with.

I'm a great fan of the concept of charging a percentage of savings, but the reality of most of those transactions suggests it's probably not nearly as good in practice as it is in concept.

If you do decide to take this route, be sure to collect a fair estimate of what that savings will be in cash, up front.

Idea #8: Upcharging for Additional Services

Not all advocates can perform all services needed by all clients. There will come a day when your client needs you to do something for him that's not in your wheelhouse.

For example: your client needs a ride to her doctor appointment. Or someone needs to pick up her new drug prescription from the pharmacy. Or she needs a medical professional to review the drugs she's taking and you don't have a medical background.

As we learned in Chapter Four, you don't just turn them away when they ask you to do something you don't do. No, instead you find someone to do it.

But you can manage the service, and be the one who bills for the service, and you can upcharge the billing. If the local medic transport costs your client $20 round trip, you can be the person who pays for it, and you can charge her $25 for it, then you pay the transport company.

However – a word of caution. Don't double dip, because that's a good way to lose trust. If you charge your client for the time it took to make the arrangements for the transportation, then don't upcharge the service, too. Do one, but not the other. And make it clear in any records how you did it, to make sure your client doesn't think you charged for it twice.

Idea #9: Increase Your Hourly Rate but Decrease Your Hours

Some advocacy services, specifically those which are not performed alongside the client, will be valued higher if they are conducted efficiently. Reviewing medical bills, coordinating Medicare services, making appointments and others – those services that require you to do some legwork behind the scenes, but not while you're talking directly to your client – your efficiency will be appreciated by your client.

When you couple this appreciation with a higher (and therefore more valued) hourly rate, you can actually make your client feel better about what it will cost to hire you, as follows:

> *Mr. Lopez, as I explain my pricing to you, let me also help you understand how I work. I'm very efficient. I have plenty of good contacts with your insurance company, and I know medical coding in my sleep. I'm a bit more expensive than many advocates, but I work much faster than they do, so the net to you for my higher level of expertise is actually a lower cost, even though I charge more per hour. I estimate it will take me 10 hours to complete this project for you, and I'll charge you $2000. Another advocate will take 15 hours to do the same thing, and will charge you more.*

Now – the truth is – it doesn't matter whether or not any of that is true. Not that you will be lying to Mr. Lopez – because he really only cares that the work gets done and favorably on his behalf. You might contract with him to finish a job in 10 hours. As long as it doesn't cost him more than you told him it would, he doesn't care if it takes you twice that.

But he will feel great – because he could afford the "more expensive" advocate who did the work for him. Your value was higher to him because he thinks you are a better, more expensive expert than someone else. In effect, you are his alligator! He'll never know that you were pulling your hair out to finish up the work in those same 15 hours it might have taken someone else.

Idea #10: Never Charge the Full Amount

Even though I've listed this as a pricing idea, please realize that it's actually more of a marketing idea. It's a simple, inexpensive idea that will put a smile on your client's face, and will boost your chances of very positive word-of-mouth marketing.

When you send a final invoice to your client, always make it a little bit less than what they expected, and call out the difference so it's right there, in their face, in black and white.

Say the contract calls for you to complete 12 hours of work for $1500. Even if it took the entire 12 hours, or a bit more, then note on the invoice that it took you 11.75 hours, then charge only $1450 – or something like that. Everyone loves to feel as if they have saved something and all you've really done is reduced your hourly rate by less than $5.

Similarly, if the scope of work changed and you went over the number of hours, but didn't ask your client for more money to cover those extra hours, make sure you note that on the invoice so they can see they actually got more than they paid for. Include an explanation that says something like "3 extra hours" – then where the dollars would go, put "No charge as per agreement" so they can see that in effect, they got a bargain.

Idea #11: Throwing in Something Extra

This idea makes your clients they feel as if they got something extra, like a gift, which then enhances what you're providing to them.

If there is a useful, quantifiable, and not time-intensive service you provide (or can develop) that you can name and offer for free – then include it in your scope of work and estimate.

For example – do you review lists of medications to be sure there are no conflicts? Or would you be able to clean out someone's medicine cabinet? What about setting them up with a spreadsheet for helping them track their medical bills? Or giving them a notebook full of special forms for tracking their daily food intake, or miles they have walked?

It's an icing-on-the-cake approach that may feel simple, like not much at all to you, but can make your client feel great about the value you've brought to the relationship. Key to making it work is including it on the invoice with "N/C" (no charge) to be sure they know it was a gift.

Idea #12: Bonus Time

Consider rewarding long-term clients for your ongoing relationship. This works well whether you've worked many hours for them, or they have had long-time retainer agreements. You'll know whether a client deserves to have a few extra hours thrown into the mix.

Should You Volunteer Your Time?

You've probably done some advocacy work for free, as a volunteer, many times for many people. Whether you come from a clinical background and you're jumping to private advocacy, or whether you just like to help people who can use your skills, many advocates (who are good-hearted people to begin with) just want to put their knowledge to work to help others.

It's noble to volunteer, of course!

But once you commit to opening your own practice, you may be getting in your own way if you volunteer your time.

As you can see from the conversations about billable hours and cash flow, it's imperative you work as many billable hours as possible. As you'll see in Chapter Nine, it will also be imperative you work on marketing your services during any time you aren't working billable hours.

Volunteer work during this time subtracts from your ability to work or market. And the truth is, as you start out, you can't afford to misuse your hours. Or, as I learned in college in Economics 101 – "opportunity lost is opportunity cost."

Commit yourself to the first few years of building your practice, then bringing in help. At the point where the income is producing itself (and it will!), THEN you'll have some spare time to pitch in to help those who really need your skills but can't afford to pay for your services.

> *"Mrs. Jacobson – we've worked together for more than six months now, and I have a policy that allows me to work the next five hours for you at no charge. You'll see those hours reflected on your next invoice."*

You might even turn the bonus time concept into a marketing idea, where you invite Mrs. Jacobson to give away some hours instead of promising them to her.

> *"Mrs. Jacobson – we've worked together for more than six months now and it's possible you have friends who might be interested in working with me, too. Here's a certificate for a free assessment (if you charge for assessments) or... Here's a certificate for three hours of my time for you to give to a friend who might be able to use my services."*

Of course, remember that the time you're promising will be non-billable time. It's actually marketing time, whether you promise it to Mrs. Jacobson or to her friend.

The bottom line to all these pricing ideas is simply to be flexible and creative, and to be sure that both you and your client feel as if your transaction is fair. There are no rules here. This is your business, and figuring out how to get paid is up to you. You can use any of these ideas, all of them, none of them, or you can combine them, even with something else.

TASK #10

Which of this ideas is attractive to you and how you'll do business?

Make some notes in your Workbook.
You'll want to review them later when you begin your work with clients.

Estimating Your Time

All these pricing ideas require you to estimate your time as accurately as you can.

Believe me when I tell you that it's almost an impossible task to estimate accurately, although you'll get better at it over time.

But there are any number of aspects of your work that will throw off any estimates you create. For example, one skill most advocates lack when they first start out is the ability to abbreviate conversations, making them effective but efficient, while still making sure the client doesn't feel as if he has been shortchanged or cut off.

You may have a pretty good idea how long it will take you to make appointments, or review a half dozen medical bills, but accounting for the conversation time that will be required to communicate that information can be an art. It will need to be adjusted according to the personality and loneliness scale of each client.

So here's some estimating and tracking advice:

- ◆ Don't forget that all estimating is one big guess. (See page 86.)

- ◆ Always estimate conservatively; that is, overestimate the amount of time the work will take you to accomplish. If it takes you less time? Great! But chances are it will take you more time.

- ◆ Try to figure out how long the actual work will take you minus discussion time (although, making phone calls and being put on hold may have to count in there, too.) Then double it. If you think the work will take you an hour, estimate two hours.

- ◆ Over time, keep track of how long certain tasks take you. Keep a log of good reference websites, or names of accountants, nursing homes, or whatever resources will help you with a future client, too. The more you keep track of good resources, the more efficient you will become.

There is no real trick to good estimating. It's not easy for anyone, and it's a skill you'll hone over time. Of course, estimating is an administrative, non-billable task, so the more efficient you become, the more billable time you'll have left over, too.

And when it comes to those long conversations many clients hope to have with you, you'll learn to make it sound as if you are the best listener in the world, even while you are moving conversations along quickly to make them more efficient.

Changes to the Scope of Work

Because advocacy is a people business, it is prone to what I call "scope creep." That is, as you move along on any given defined project, one in which you have a contract in place that defines what's expected to be done in how many hours for how much money, there is a tendency for clients to begin asking for more than what's in that agreement.

For example, Mrs. Murray has asked you to sort, review and negotiate her insurance bills. You begin with an agreement that you'll handle all the bills that arrive in February. But March 3rd, another one comes in, and she asks you if you'll add that to the list, too.

OK. So one extra isn't a big deal. But then she asks you to add the one that comes in on the 5th. What should you do? After all – you gave a centimeter. Mrs. Murray is working on her entire kilometer.

I know of one advocate who was doing such a good job for her client, that her client handed over all her sister's bills, too – and got upset with the advocate for suggesting that her sister's bills weren't part of their agreement! That tells us that the agreement should have been more carefully written, but also that it was an unacceptable expectation, too.

There are a few things you can do to professionally handle this kind of situation. It requires balancing your relationship with making sure no one is taking advantage of your generosity.

You might tell Mrs. Murray that you are happy to add one bill to the pile, but if a second one comes in, you'll ask her to extend your contract – in effect, adding to your scope of work and expected payment.

You might ask Mrs. Murray that since she must see the value of the good work you are doing (after all, she did ask you to do more!), wouldn't she like to sign a retainer agreement so all the bills are just handed over to you for the next.. oh… year?

In any case that begins to look like scope creep, be sure to raise the situation as soon as you recognize it with your client. Don't be afraid to explain – early – that something is outside your scope, and try to use the situation to your advantage to either renegotiate your contract, or start with a new, expanded one.

When to Ask for Your Money

There is only one answer to this question about when to ask a client for money. The answer is "up front."

I've written that. You've read that. But I guarantee you that someday you will have a client who doesn't pay you up front, you'll do some of the work, but you'll get stiffed for payment.

Be warned. It happens to everyone. It's like a rite of passage. It has happened to me, and it will likely happen to you, too. Just don't let it happen twice.

We all want to think that the people who will choose to work with us are good-hearted, paying souls. And I think they are, for the most part. It's just that some of them are good hearted, with good intentions, but not enough money.

Bounced checks. Promised checks that never appear. They are far too common.

That's why it's imperative you get your money up front, why you wait for checks to clear, or why you only accept credit cards (which will get rejected immediately if there's not enough of a credit limit.)

When you begin working with a client to do an assessment or to develop your scope of work, make it clear from the get-go that you'll expect the money up front.

If you'll be working with a retainer agreement, then you will bill one month ahead, and two months up front. (Your contract begins in April, so you bill for April and May at the start, expecting May payment by April 30. Then on May 1, you bill for June, expecting payment by May 31, and so forth.)

If you'll be working on a long term project basis, you might break up a large total into halves or thirds, but make sure you get paid for the next part of the project before you begin working on it.

> *"So now that we've discussed and agreed on the scope of work, Mrs. Michaels, let's discuss payment. As you see in the terms of my agreement, I expect payment up front. Would you like to pay me by credit card? Or would you prefer to write a check?"*

The bottom line is that the road to advocacy heaven is paved with good client intentions. There will be times when you are tempted to forego payment when you know someone needs you. (Maybe they are hospitalized, or they go off on vacation and forget to pay you but you know they have an appointment the day they get home and want you to go with them....) The reasons are as vast as the payments they haven't made. You'll have to make a judgment call at the time.

But if you let too many clients make excuses, there will be someone who doesn't pay you. That might include a client who dies before writing you a check!

Manage their expectations about payment well, so they will know to pay you when the money is due and will make sure you are paid on time. That's good, smart business.

Sure! Go ahead!
This is a blank page, and it's
your book, so make some notes...

Chapter Nine
Marketing Your Advocacy Services

All those pages that focus on money always make me nervous. It's definitely more fun to think about all the money we'll bring in (certainly more fun than all that money it will cost us to be in business) - until the realization hits: just who will pay us all that money?

The "who" is the question that is answered by marketing. Marketing simply means you're going to find the right people and you're going to help them understand the benefits of hiring you – so they will.

It sounds simple! And really – it can be. The key is to approach it by understanding what you're doing, why you're doing it, how to do it – and then (as Larry the Cable Guy says) "git 'er done!"

As we go through the next many pages of marketing, I have a confession to make to you.... That is – been there and done that. Prior to putting together this handbook for you, I wrote *The Health Advocate's Marketing Handbook*. It's a comprehensive look at marketing for private advocacy practices and will not be replicated here. Instead, this chapter will provide some of the most basic information about marketing your practice.

Once you are ready to take a deeper dive into marketing, *The Health Advocate's Marketing Handbook* will be far more useful. (Find purchase information in the Resources section in the back of this book.)

Why Will People Want to Hire You?

The healthcare system has evolved to become so extremely difficult to manage that few individuals, in particular when they are sick or overwhelmed, can manage to get what they need from it, at a fair cost in energy or money.

This evolution (or perhaps, more like, "devolution") has come about for a variety of reasons. We actually covered these points quite closely in the Introduction to this book.

(If you want a quick refresher, return to the Introduction. Take your time. I'll wait....)

The bottom line is that all those reasons have created a perfect storm of need on the part of sick or injured people, and that need can be filled by health advocates.

Marketing 101 – a Few Basics

In its simplest form, marketing is simply the education aspect of business – teaching the right people that you have the ability and availability to fill their need – either with a product or a service.

Marketing isn't exactly the same as sales but it's very closely related. Marketing provides the tools to make sales happen. In a large corporation, they are two different but related departments, with different staffs and different responsibilities. In a small business, like your advocacy practice, marketing and sales are so intertwined that you'd be hard pressed to know when you're doing which.

In an advocacy practice, the "sale" is engagement – it's the point when your potential client turns into a contracted client, with a signature and a check.

So that's the goal for our marketing (and sales) – to support, encourage, and foster that engagement.

The foundation for good marketing is comprised of six steps. Each one is explained in much more depth in this chapter.

1. **Listing your products / services**: What do you offer that people want and need?
2. **Identifying your target audiences**: Who will hire you to perform those services? Who will actually write you a check?
3. **Developing your messages**: What do your target audiences want and need to know to help them decide to write you that check?
4. **Creating your strategy**: how will you deliver those messages to the target audiences you've identified and what will you ask them to do?
5. **Executing your strategy and tactics**: delivering your messages to your target audiences, then managing their response.
6. **Measuring your marketing outreach**: gauging your success, and regrouping if necessary.

1. Listing your products / services: What do you offer that people want and need?

In Chapter Four, you did a good analysis of what your skills are, and what services you want to offer. In Task #4 in your workbook, you recorded your choices.

So the thinking you'll need to put into this step is already finished.

TASK #11

Return to Task #4, and bring your ideas forward to the
marketing section of your workbook.
You may even give some second thought to your services
now that you've read more of this book.

2. Identifying your target audiences: Who will hire you to perform those services? Who will actually write you a check?

Here is where we begin to create profiles of exactly the people we know will want to use our services. Their profiles will include as many details as we can describe so that later, when we work on our messages, we can craft them to be understandable by these folks.

There is one important attribute to call to your attention that will be true for all of them: That is, in all cases, every single target audience or potential client must have enough savings or disposable income to pay you. Of 10 people who call or email to inquire about your services, at least half of them won't have money to pay you. They will believe that you should work for them for free (usually because they think that insurance makes all the rest of their healthcare 'free'). But you don't "owe" them free services any more than a lawyer or hairdresser or car mechanic owes his or her clients free services. So, part of our description of every target audience includes the ability to afford to hire you.

One additional distinction to make; That is, that your "client" is the person who pays you. Your "patient" (a word we actually avoid – see the Sidebar in Chapter Four) – might be the person you perform services for, but that person may not be the person who pays you. Our target audiences are all either the people who will actually pay us, or they are the people who will influence someone else to pay us.

Here are some target audience profile examples to help you better understand:

1. Seniors: male or female, chronic conditions or new (scary) diagnoses like cancer, heart disease, COPD, diabetes or others, facing big changes in their lives based on treatment needs (chemo, surgery, others), with the means to pay us for our work.

2. Adult children: male or female, often live too far away to be regular caregivers, trying to balance life (marriage, kids, work) with making sure Mom or Dad gets what he/she needs, who want us to be feet-on-the-ground when the parent needs assistance, with the means to pay us for our work.

3. The Elderly: male or female, debilitated either mentally or physically or both. Often these folks are "influencers," meaning they may not pay us themselves, but will suggest to their adult child, who they THINK have the means to pay us, to get in touch with us to help.

4. Media: You may be surprised to see this audience, but media are definitely influencers, and to the extent you're willing to reach out and be interviewed, or to write a column, or to end up in their rolodex of experts, you can do a lot of marketing through media. In order to target them, you'll develop specific messages for them, which we will do shortly.

5. Other influencers include attorneys (eldercare, wills and estates, trusts), hospital or rehab center discharge planners, guardians or conservators, church or synagogue congregants, employers, union leaders, and personnel who work for home healthcare companies.

You may be able to determine additional target audiences for your practice, especially if you are working toward developing a niche. (And, as mentioned before, *The Health Advocate's Marketing Handbook* has much more on this topic.)

TASK #12

Who are your target audiences? Record them.

---

3. Developing your messages: What do your target audiences want and need to know to help them decide to write you that check?

Most marketing newbies think this step is quite easy... all one needs to do is make a list of services and clients will flock to their phones, right?

No. Not right. While that may work on occasion, there is a far better approach. That is, we are going to put ourselves in our target audience's shoes, and then create a list of benefits to working with us that will push each target audience's buttons. Not so simple – but definitely more fruitful.

We'll begin with WHY they want and need to hire you. The answer to that question is based on their emotional state, and their point-of-view, and not framed the way you frame your services.

The FUD Theory

FUD = fear, uncertainty and doubt. In a nutshell, with perhaps some guilt thrown in (but YOU try adding a G to that nice little acronym), the FUD theory explains why probably 92.6% of people reach out to us to inquire about working with us.

Fear – because they have been dealt a set of circumstances they don't understand and are afraid will change, ruin or end their lives, affecting their health or their finances or both.

Uncertainty – because that fear impairs their ability to think straight, to cope with their new circumstances. Further, they realize they don't know the system – the right people or resources to fix it for them.

Doubt – because they doubt their own ability to fix the problem, to manage it on their own, successfully, without ruining or ending their lives, their health and their finances.

Guilt – This isn't its own attribute; rather it colors the others in some circumstances, in particular when the client is one person and the actual patient is another. Adult children who live too far away and think they should be doing something to help out may hire an advocate because they feel guilty – but it's only the icing on top of the FUD cake.

So what alleviates their FUD? Finding someone else they can trust to fix it for them. Once we understand that trust is at the root of hiring decisions, then we can use that to develop our messages for each group.

Exactly what do they need to know to trust you? Here are some of the attributes that prove you are trustworthy and will lead to your being hired. They want to know you are, or have:

- **Know-how or ability**: You are capable of fixing their problem or at least making it easier to weather.

- **Experience**: You have fixed similar problems for other people before.

- **Resourceful**: You have access to the resources necessary to fix their problem and the creativity to find new ones.

- **A good communicator**: That you are easy to talk to and have a pleasant personality – because in a state of FUD, they don't want to deal with someone who is difficult to understand.

- **Affordable**: Not in terms of dollars, but when compared to the alternative. If the alternative is choosing the wrong treatment which could debilitate them for the rest of (what could amount to) a very short life, they will find a way to afford you.

- **Available**: Either in person, or by phone, or online, or in whatever way makes the most sense for their circumstances.

Peace of Mind

FUD and guilt are quite easy to understand. Realizing that clients want and need to be able to trust is not a stretch from there. Now let's add them together. What do we get when we relieve FUD and show that we are trustworthy?

We begin to provide potential clients with peace of mind. Like the hero on the white horse, when we show up while they are feeling fearful, uncertain and doubtful, representing the skills they need, and the ability to take responsibility on their behalf... that gives them a a huge sense of relief, and fulfills their much-needed wish for peace of mind.

Focus on Benefits

Now that we better understand a potential client's point of view, including their pursuit of peace of mind, let's take a look at your services and figure out how to describe them by leveraging that point of view.

Let's say that one service you offer is to review a client's medications. Here are different ways to describe that service:

(1) Medication Review	(2) Review of medications to be sure there are no conflicts.	(3) Review of medications to be sure conflicts aren't causing symptoms.

If you were in a potential client's shoes, which of these is more likely to encourage you to make contact with the person offering the service? Which one will provide you with some sense of peace of mind?

Of course, number 3, maybe even number 2. Both offer a service, combined with the potential for peace of mind.

The reason #2 and #3 work better is because they focus on the benefit to the client, rather than the service itself. They answer the question about why a medication review would be important, and #3 even suggests that the patient's symptoms might be fairly simply eliminated if conflicts are identified.

Other examples of focusing on benefits —for mediation services:

(1) Interviewing all family members involved	(2) Interviewing all family members involved to be sure their interests are recorded

... or for medical bill reviewers:

(1) Organization of medical bills	(2) Organization of medical bills to be sure no duplicate billing is taking place

Managing Expectations

It should probably go without saying that you want to be sure your messages are a close reflection of what a client can expect, and that you don't promise more than you can deliver. But let's frame this message from the client's point of view, too....

When anyone is FUD, then they are usually desperate, too. And through desperation, they don't hear words with the same objective clarity they might otherwise hear them. They may leap to conclusions that just aren't true.

Whether you have a conversation with them, or if they read something on your website or your Facebook page, or pick up a brochure after you've spoken to their group – do your best to be clear about your deliverables, without letting them make assumptions that you never intended.

You may say the words, "We'll get you a second opinion." But they may hear, "A second opinion will make the first, bad diagnosis go away." You may say to them, "I'll review your hospital bill to see if we can lower it," and they may hear, "Your hospital bill is wrong and I'm going to save you lots of money."

One of the most important pieces of advice I can give you for any aspect of your business is to clearly manage their expectations – both good and bad. Your declaration should be, "We'll get you a second opinion to either confirm the one you've gotten or to see if there are alternatives to consider." Or, "I'll review your hospital bill for accuracy."

> **LUCKY TASK #13**
>
> For each of your services, write up 2-3 possible benefits statements
> that incorporate the service itself, but even more so,
> the point of view of a potential client.

Your Elevator Pitch

One specific message you should develop is called a positioning statement, or more affectionately, an elevator pitch. An elevator pitch is a 15-30 second description of what you do for a living. The idea is that, if you got into an elevator on the first floor and started describing your business to the other person in the elevator, you would complete the description before you reached the top floor.

There is a fairly simple formula for putting together your elevator pitch. Once you've determined what it will be, then begin practicing it to be sure it rolls off your tongue.

TASK #14

Develop your elevator pitch.
You'll find the formula in your Workbook.

4. Creating your strategy: how will you deliver those messages to the target audiences you've identified, and what will you ask them to do?

Once you know exactly who your target audiences are, and what messages you want them to hear or see, then it's time to put together a good strategy for getting the word out.

Strategy is the big picture of creating your brand, prioritizing your target audiences, and choosing the tactics to reach them.

Branding

Among the most important components of your strategy will be your brand. While most of us think of a brand as a logo, it's really much more than that. It's the message that goes with that logo telling people what they can expect when they see it or hear about your brand.

For example, what do you think of when you hear "McDonalds"? Or see those golden arches? You think about fast food, relatively inexpensive, geared toward families and kids (although happy to have anyone eat there), usually very clean, and always consistent – and you think of that whether you see those arches in California or Nova Scotia or anywhere in between.

But what do you think of when you hear "Ferdinand's Steakhouse"? Probably nothing... Because that's not a brand that's familiar to you. You don't know anything about it. No logo comes to mind, but also, you don't have any idea how the food tastes, how pricey it might be, how friendly the waitstaff is, whether or not the restrooms are clean – nuttin.

So the first strategy you'll want to develop is your brand. Your name, your logo, your business personality (professional, friendly, helpful, etc), and perhaps even a tag line, plus a description of exactly what you want people to think of when they hear or see your company name or see your logo.

If you have any graphic design ability, then go ahead and give it a try yourself. But if not, or if you don't have confidence in your abilities, then by all means, hire a graphic designer to develop your logo. Make sure he or she understands your brand personality and designs something to your personality. Even if you have favorite colors, consider not sharing those colors to see what the designer comes up with, because colors have psychological influences and a good designer will take those into account when creating your logo and the other graphic pieces of your brand.

Tactics Are Marketing Tools

Tactics are all those things you've heard of: advertising, public relations, brochures, speaking, newsletters and many more. Tactics are the tools you use to execute the strategy. Tactics will always reflect your brand.

Just like building a house or fixing a car requires different tools for different aspects of the job, the job of marketing requires different tactics for different aspects, too.

Overcoming Objections

Most people who voice objections to any aspect of your work – from the services you provide to what you charge – might be voicing objections because they really wish they could hire you.

It seems counter-intuitive, doesn't it? But here's an example:

Think back to when you were 8 years old and you didn't get invited to a birthday party that you thought you should have been invited to. Your response? "I didn't really want to go anyway!" Clearly there was a disconnect between your hurt, and the words you spoke.

And so it is in business. One of the objections I hear most frequently is, "Oh, so only people with money can hire you." Or, "Oh, so you have to be rich to have an advocate help you."

Of course, neither of those statements are true – but since they are frequent objections, it's best we know exactly what our response will be when we hear them. Think of objections as an opportunity to expand your marketing. Tap into the objector's point of view.

A reply might be, "Actually – when you consider the alternative, like the numbers of medical errors, or drug conflicts, or overpayment on hospital bills, or death – my services are quite inexpensive." (OK, so maybe you don't want to mention death – but you get the point.)

Another might be, "I actually offer a number of different packages so my services end up being quite affordable." Or "Mr. Henry, the cost to hire me is a small price to pay for peace of mind."

If you begin to hear similar objections about any aspect of your practice, write them down, and prepare your response ahead of time so that next time you'll know exactly what to say.

For example: if you've just hired a new advocate to work in your business, you might issue a press release about it (that's public relations), but you probably wouldn't run a display ad in a newspaper. You'd probably add him or her to your website, and even announce the engagement on your Facebook page. You'd print up business cards and mention it in a newsletter, but you wouldn't put up a billboard.

Each of those tools has a purpose, an audience, a time (calendar time) and a cost. Some of them cost your time (in hours), some cost money, some cost time and money. The idea in strategy development is to weigh the audiences, the messages, the calendar and the cost to determine which ones will be most effective at the least cost.

Here are some of the tactics you might choose from, all inexpensive in money-cost, some a bit more involved in time-cost, all highly effective in reaching your target audiences with your messages:

Word of Mouth

Bar none, word of mouth (WOM) is the most powerful type of marketing there is. When someone who is respected by others says something good about your work and you, then you have just won the superbowl of marketing. That one good thing that person said is more powerful, and will have a bigger effect on your success than running a thousand dollars-worth of advertisements.

You can encourage word-of-mouth. First, by always being highly professional and delivering what you promise, on time, for the agreed upon amount of money.

And second, by "making the ask" – by asking a client at the end of your relationship, "Would you be willing to endorse my work?" Or, "Would you write me a letter of recommendation that I may use in my marketing?" (If you are listed in the AdvoConnection Directory, your testimonial can also be added to your directory listing.)

Public Speaking

If you are comfortable speaking in front of groups of people, large or small, then public speaking is a great way to garner trust and impart good information. Local seniors groups, the Rotary Club's lunch meeting, your Chamber of Commerce; most of these groups are looking for speakers and will happily add you to their roster once they know you have a program of interest.

That's the key for these public speaking gigs – the right program. Your topic should not be about private advocacy, per se. Instead, you'll want to choose a topic that is current or useful, in which you can weave the smart idea of hiring a private advocate. For example, you can talk about what Medicare recipients can expect from the Affordable Care Act's changes to the donut hole. Or you could address "How to Stay Safe in the Hospital" where

Should You Include Pricing on Your Website?

I wish I had a definitive answer for you on this question; I don't.

But I can give you some food for thought, and perhaps an approach to figure out for yourself whether you should include pricing on your website.

In Chapter Eight, page 95, I suggested you never offer your hourly rate as an isolated piece of information. You don't want someone dismissing the possibility of working with you because they leap to conclusions about whether they can afford your services.

That said, if we look at pricing models in other market sectors, we find that including a price, whether or not it's entirely accurate, will increase sales. For example, think about purchasing a used car from the newspaper classifieds. If the price was there, and it seemed fair, then you would call the number. If no price was included, you'd just move on.

Most advocates I know do not include pricing on their websites. Since there is so little competition for their services, they are getting calls anyway. But I've seen pricing on the websites of several well-known, busy advocates, too.

If you feel strongly about including the pricing, consider using some examples of your work, or describe your packages and price them favorably, but with a disclaimer that they are representative only and any individual's pricing would not be the same.

One other idea – you can simply make a statement that says "Contact us for pricing. We're far more affordable than you might expect!" At least that suggests that you're not trying to take their last dime.

you focus on avoiding infection, falls and drug errors. Of course, professional health advocates are a vital part of solutions for each.

Public speaking has a great ripple effect, too. If there are 50 people in the room, then they will mention your talk to 50 more, who might mention it to 50 more.

An important key to success with public speaking: Be sure to provide each attendee with a handout that lists your benefits messages, and provides your phone number, email address, web address, Facebook page and anything else they might want to access and peruse. Be sure your handout (and your slides if you make up a powerpoint presentation) reflect your branding. And don't forget your call to action (described later in this chapter.)

Marketing on the Web

As offerings on the Web continue to evolve, new web tools become available, too. A few short years ago, we were limited to "surfing" websites. Today we have websites, blogs, directories, and social media options that range from Twitter to Facebook to Pinterest. By the time you read this book, there will be new possibilities we haven't yet fathomed.

Of dozens of ideas, and hundreds of options, no matter what comes down the pike in the near future, there are two keys to maximizing your marketing on the web:

1. Create a web presence: Starting right out, a website is a must, even if it's only one page. It shows that you are serious, that you are professional, and that you've taken the time to be sure you are available for people to find you. It also reflects your brand. (Which also means you may need a professional to help you with it to be sure it is recognizable as part of your brand.)

Early in your business marketing, and later as time allows, participation in social media, such as Facebook, Twitter, Pinterest or LinkedIn will be vital, too. The key is to maximize your web presence, and to make it easy to reach out to you.

2. Make yourself more easily findable on the web: Your website presence won't do you much good if no one finds you. There are two things you can do to make yourself more findable.

One is to pepper your website, and any other web presence, with keywords – those words someone will use to search for you. "Health advocate, patient navigator, [your location, city and state], cancer, mediation, doula..." whatever words your potential clients will use when they go looking for advocacy help. These words must appear on your site because they will be "crawled" by search engines (Google, Yahoo, Bing and others.) Then, when someone who needs you goes in search of you using their own words, you will be found in the search results.

The second is to then make sure that there are many links elsewhere on the web that link back to your website. Note – these are not links that go from your site to others. They are links that come back to you. Search engines look at how many links come TO your site as a measure of your authority. The more links TO you, the more authority they assign to you, and the closer to the top of a search you will be.

Begin by making sure all your web presences link to all others. Link your website to your LinkedIn and Facebook pages. Link your social media pages back to your website, too. Then look for opportunities outside your own presence to create links back to your sites. Comment on other people's blog posts and include your web address with your signature, ask Facebook friends to link to you from their pages, join APHA as a Premium member once you've launched your practice (you'll be in the directory that links back to your website). Look for new opportunities to amass links back to your website and social media pages.

There are so many ways to expand your marketing outreach on the web, that there are entire books written on just this topic alone. Jump in as much as you're willing and able to use this important tool to promote your practice.

Collateral

The term collateral refers to anything that's printed with the intent of giving it away, like your business cards, flyers, or brochures.

Business cards are a must, professionally branded, of course. Give them to everyone you meet.

Other collateral can be made up as you need it, and with today's easy print technology at places like FedEx Kinkos or Staples, you can print as many as you need and no more. Ask your designer to develop a template you can use on your computer to fill in or edit with the information you want to include, then print off as you need it. That's an inexpensive way to develop plenty of professional collateral material.

Public Relations

Do you ever wonder how the newspaper or TV news know about all the community-type news the tell you about? How did they know there was a fundraiser for that poor girl who got hit by a car? Or that festival that's taking place in town next weekend? Or that Kathy Miller was promoted to president of the bank?

The answer is: public relations, most likely in the form of press releases. Someone working on that fundraiser, or that festival, or the PR department at the bank issued a press release which told what the event was, who was involved, its purpose, why it was important for the public to know about it, and more.

You, too, can issue a press release. It's one of the easiest forms of marketing, and costs no more than a little bit of time.

It's a great way to announce to the world that you are in business, that you've started your private practice. Using email, just write up the details, and send it to all your local print publications, from daily newspapers to weekly tabloids. Some, not all, will print it. You'll be surprised at how many will see it. It's a great way to kick off your business. Be sure to include your headshot (professional photo) with it, too.

A sample press release is contained both in the membership space at APHA, and in The Health Advocate's Marketing Handbook. But you can also just go online and search for a basic press release template if you need a guideline.

Call to Action

With the possible exception of your business cards and your branding, every other marketing tactic should include a call-to-action.

A call to action is a way of telling a potential client what to do if they want to benefit from working with you. "Call us!" Or "Email us!" "Call today for a no-obligation assessment." Such instructions should be found on every page of your online / web presence, every brochure or flyer—everything.

Just be sure to make it easy for them to do what they've been told. If you tell them to call you, put your phone number right there. Same with your email address.

What About Market Research?

If you pick up a formal marketing textbook, or talk to a high-end marketing consultant, they will tell you that doing research is actually the starting point for your marketing; indeed, that it's the starting point for determining whether or not to even start a practice. Some would chastise me for burying market research in the ninth chapter of this book – that determining one's audience, under the guise of "market research," should be front and center and every other business decision should be based on it.

Baloney, I say! Well, baloney for most of us... with a few exceptions....

I do agree that having a good handle on who your target audiences are is very important, as discussed here. However, market research is not just about who your audiences are, but how many of them there are. They believe you need to know that before you think about going into business for yourself, because if there aren't enough people to pay you for your services, then going into business doesn't make any sense.

If your idea is to open an advocacy business on a grand scale, hiring dozens, if not hundreds of others to work for you to serve the needs of your community, state or country – well, then – they are right. Do that research.

Also, if you have determined that you want to fulfill a very specific niche, and you want to do that in a small population area, then yes – they are right about doing research to determine numbers, too. One potential advocate asked me about working only with patients with a specific sort of unusual brain tumor. He lives in an area of fewer than 50,000 people. Unless his community is built on top of a toxic waste dump, that probably won't work. Market research would likely tell him to expand his geography, or broaden his services.

This book is focused on opening a smaller, more general practice. Not that you can't begin working toward a niche, but as we determined in Chapter Four, if your geographic or population area is smaller, you may need to expand your practice, or expand your geography to fill your time and your income needs.

One other point about research: It would actually be almost impossible to do it accurately. The profession of health advocacy is too new to be able to know, for example, what percentage of people between the ages of 55 and 68 might hire us, despite the fact that it would be very possible to figure out how often they eat hamburgers, or go to the movies.

As the number of advocates grows, and as the profession becomes more recognized, large research groups may be able to figure out some numbers we can use. But for today, your success won't be based on whether research determines there are large numbers of people who might hire you because there's not enough competition or definition.

We do know that almost anyone who needs a doctor needs an advocate, too. That's all the market research most of us need for now.

As far as those forms that you can put on your website—as stand alones, they are not good enough. If someone is FUD, and they come across a contact form on your website-they're gone. If you insist on using a form, make sure your phone number and/or email address are available, too.

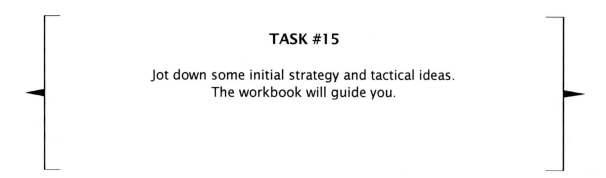

TASK #15

Jot down some initial strategy and tactical ideas.
The workbook will guide you.

5. Executing your strategy and tactics: delivering your messages to your target audiences, then managing their response.

The execution of your strategy – using your tactics (tools) – will take place when you begin to do outreach for your new practice. You may actually begin doing some of it before you officially start your business. Word of mouth is a great place to begin.

The only advice here is to get at it. Start marketing early and often. We've reviewed and developed the basics. It's up to you to make them happen.

6. Measuring your marketing outreach: gauging your success, and regrouping if necessary.

A famous retailer named John Wanamaker once said that he knew that 50 percent of his advertising worked, he just wasn't sure which 50 percent.

That's how you'll feel about a lot of your marketing, too. You may give away 100 business cards, and one person will call you. Or you may speak to a large group of seniors, and you'll get a half dozen calls. None of them will have attended your talk – but they heard from someone who heard from someone else, who talked to her sister-in-law.... Etc.

Why measure your marketing? Because it will help you decide which tactics are working and which aren't. In particular for the marketing that costs you a lot of money or time, you can step up your efforts (if you determine they are working well) or stop doing them all together (if you decide they are a waste of time.)

Some of your marketing effectiveness can be measured quite easily. If you issue a press release, and it shows up in the newspaper on Tuesday, then your phone begins to ring Tuesday afternoon, then you know your efforts were worthwhile.

Web traffic can be measured through analytics (ask your web developer.) Facebook will tell you how many "likes" you're getting. Asking someone for a testimonial, then hearing from his friend – that's an easy measurement.

Good marketing requires lots of repetition, because it's plenty of repetition that causes someone to remember your brand. The accepted maxim within marketing is that it takes seven to nine exposures before someone remembers your brand. So don't dismiss tactics too quickly. If you issue 10 press releases and never get a phone call, then it's time to hang up your press release gloves – but not before.

Finally, remember that marketing doesn't stop for any individual client once you have a contract signed. Marketing takes place throughout your work with them, through good customer service, managing expectations throughout the relationship, and once you and your client have finished your work together, asking them to help you with your marketing.

No, you won't ask them to do that in so many words. Instead, you'll ask them to provide an endorsement for your work, or you may want to survey them about their experience working with you. You'll leave behind some of your brochures and business cards when you're finished, and a few weeks later you'll follow up with them, just to make sure things are going well (because if they aren't, you may have another opportunity to work with them.)

The Marketing Dance

The elements of a good dance are very similar to the elements of good marketing. Someone must lead (you, the business owner), and someone must follow (clients, as they contact you). Sometimes the dance is faster and more complex, sometimes it's slower and less challenging. And of course, you must keep dancing as long as the music is playing (or as long as you are in business).

Throughout your ownership of your practice, you'll need to continue marketing. Initially it will require the bulk of your time while you garner new clients. But, once you have clients, please don't forget that the music is still playing! One day those clients will no longer be clients, and unless you've kept up with your marketing, you won't have anyone to work with, and you won't have an income.

Commit yourself to some amount of marketing every day, even if it's just checking in on your Facebook page, or returning a few inquiries through email. Always return phone calls or email to potential (and current) clients as quickly as you can, as well as any inquiries from the media.

Be sure you keep doing that marketing dance, or you'll run the risk of having no work just when you have the available billable hours available to do it.

Be Prepared for the Results of Good Marketing

Of course, the goal for all your marketing is to make your phone ring – to bring you new clients. As long as you've carefully and accurately created your brand, described your target audiences, developed your messages, and executed your strategy well, your phone will ring – and you need to be prepared.

This, too, is part of the marketing dance; making sure you never have more partners than you can handle. You'll want to balance your marketing efforts to bring you more clients when you have the time to work with more of them, and to slow down new inquiries when you know your time is already committed to the clients you already have.

For the first year or two of business, you'll find that your feast and famine days are far too common. You'll either be busier than you want to be, or not busy enough. Once you've

▲

Independent Contractors Need Marketing, Too

Marketing is marketing, and the basics are the same, whether you plan to work for clients directly, or whether you'll be hired by other advocates or advocacy companies as an independent contractor.

If your goal is to subcontract only, then nothing you've read in this chapter changes; it simply gets adjusted.

Further, your knowledge of good marketing will add value to your services when another advocate or an advocacy company considers hiring you.

If you go through the tasks in this marketing chapter, you'll see that they are the same – but adjusted for YOUR target audience – another advocate.

Where are those advocates? How do you find them?

What services will you offer them, and even more importantly, how will they benefit from hiring you to provide those services?

How will you deliver your marketing messages to them, and how will you measure the effectiveness of your outreach?

The basic principles of marketing apply to you and your work, no matter who will write you a check, even if you decide after all this that you'd just as soon work in a hospital, or for an insurance company.

A benefits-focused resume is always a winner.

▼

gotten more used to the rhythm of business, you'll know when it's time to gear up to do more public speaking or even some advertising. You'll also know when to back off those marketing tasks a little to give yourself a breather.

And, too, you'll begin to have a sense of when it's time to bring in help. At the point when you know that your business is growing, despite the fact that you are doing only that baseline level of marketing, then it will be time to think about bringing in some freelancers / subcontractors to help you out.

Or not. You may just as well decide that it's time to begin turning away some clients, referring them to another advocate who can help them, and even raising your rates so as to deter those you don't want to work with.

But that will be then, and this is now.

Get your marketing started and stand by – your phone is about to ring!

Chapter Ten
Protecting Yourself and Your Business: Legal and Insurance Considerations

When I was a teenager, I knew exactly what career I wanted. I wanted to be an elementary school teacher. But my father thought I should be a lawyer.

"You have a sense of fairness and an analytical mind," he told me. "Why don't you study law? You'd make a great lawyer!"

But I had no interest in studying the law. I remember telling Dad, "Why would I want to spend my life fixing other people's arguments, or trying to prevent them to begin with? I've got enough arguments of my own without trying to get in the middle of someone else's." [13]

Still today, as a lifelong Pollyanna, I feel that same way, both about the world of law, and its partner-in-backside-coverage, insurance. The entire idea behind both of them is about blame, fault, and making someone else pay – OR – preventing any of those three.

Now – don't get me wrong.... I totally understand the necessity of having both lawyers and insurers, and value my relationships with the ones I work with. Just because I don't want to do what they do for a living doesn't diminish their importance. Nor does it diminish my appreciation for the fact that they can both keep me out of hot water, and temper that same water if I get into trouble.

Among most of the advocates and soon-to-be-advocates I have met, most are just like me – Pollyannas in our hearts. And while Pollyannaism serves us well in many aspects of our lives, when it comes to our businesses, we need to learn to put her on a shelf, walk away, and gulp down a broad reality check.

---

13 Yes, I did go on to be an elementary teacher – a career that spanned 10 years. After that, after moving to a new state, I couldn't get a new teaching job because too much experience and education made me too expensive! That's when I changed careers to marketing. And 20+ years after that, patient empowerment and advocacy. I've always credited my teaching and marketing background for helping me do the work I do today.

So why do I explain all of this? Because, unless you are a lawyer or an insurer, I'm guessing that you feel similarly about legal and insurance matters. While our perfect worlds would mean neither would have to exist, we can at least appreciate that they are there when we need them to protect us.

In our roles as business / practice owners, we just cannot afford to be Pollyannas.

What Can Go Wrong Will Go Wrong

Consider:

Marvin Malone's advocate, Melanie Murphy, is an RN with a certificate in patient navigation from XYZ University. She has coordinated Mr. Malone's care on and off for almost a year. One of her favorite parts of her work was getting to know not just Mr. Malone, but his family, too – his wife of 50+ years, his adult daughter and two of his grandchildren.

About six months ago, Mr. Malone was admitted to the hospital. The family opted not to hire Melanie to provide bedside advocacy services, but Melanie visited Mr. Malone in the hospital each day because she wanted to – she had grown close to him.

About a week into his stay, Mr. Malone needed to use the bathroom in the middle of the night. He pushed the call button many times, but no one arrived to help. He finally edged out of his bed on his own, and (you knew this was coming...) he collapsed just steps from the bed, breaking his arm and collarbone.

After Mr. Malone's discharge, the family filed a lawsuit against the hospital for not responding to Mr. Malone's call, causing him to fall. Without the family's knowledge, the lawyers added Melanie's advocacy practice to the list of professionals they sued.

Now Melanie, through no mistake or fault of her own, must hire a lawyer to defend herself against something she wasn't involved in. She's feeling particularly stunned because she felt her relationship with both Mr. Malone and his family was very strong.

Or consider:

Jason, the owner of Bust Those Bills Medical Billing Reviewers, was invited to be interviewed on his local TV station during the 6:30am news on a Tuesday morning. During the interview, he was asked many questions about how he works miracles with medical bills, and highlighted one story about a family who had almost gone bankrupt from the bills they accumulated after the husband fell off the roof trying to replace a shingle that had blown off during a storm. He had managed to cut their bills down to a fraction of the original total and claimed he had saved them more than $50,000.

Several months later, after working with a client to reduce his wife's hospital bills, the client sued Jason for false advertising because he had only lopped about $12,000 of their bills. The client claimed he had hired Jason because he thought Jason would cut at least $50,000 based on the TV interview.

Now Jason must hire a lawyer to defend a lawsuit that will probably be thrown out... but he must incur that legal expense anyway.

Or consider:

Laurie Littleton offers family mediation services, specifically to families in crisis over a loved one's health challenges, which usually means the adult children—siblings--are arguing over whether Dad needs to go into a nursing home and whether they should sell Dad's house to pay for it – or some similar crisis.

And so it was with this particular case. Laurie contracted with a family of six siblings, three of whom live out of state, two of whom don't want Dad's house sold (because they want to wait until he dies so they can get their piece of the inheritance) and one of whom has been doing all the caregiving. Laurie's contract calls for 20 hours of mediation services, resulting in a final report of all the decisions made, and how those decisions will be executed.

A meeting among all six siblings was set up for a Thursday evening in the home of the oldest brother who lives in the next town over from Laurie. The plan includes using a conference phone line so the out-of-town siblings could participate, too. Since one of the sisters lives right on the way, Laurie offers to pick her up so they can drive together.

But when they arrive, the oldest brother gets all bent out of shape because he translates Laurie's transportation offer to mean she is biased toward the sister who rode with her. As the discussion of sticking points ensues, that brother becomes more and more belligerent because he feels as if he isn't being listened to. Eventually, keeping her cool, Laurie suggests they convene at another time, that she will draw up the notes from that evening's conversation, and it will give them a platform for picking up the next part of the conversation....

But the next morning, she gets an email from that brother telling her she's been fired and that because of her bias toward the one sister, they will not even pay for the services rendered to that point.

Now Laurie must figure out whether she can collect the money due, and/or how to smooth over the brother's ruffled feathers.

....

Do any of these scenarios surprise you? Many new advocates, particularly the Pollyannas among us, find it hard to grasp that these kinds of situations could ever befall someone who only wants to provide good services to deserving people with the best intentions.

And, I'm at least pleased to tell you that, as of this book going to press (Fall 2012) I know of no practicing advocates who have run into these problems so far. (That doesn't mean they haven't happened – I just don't know about them.) Among those of us who attempt to think ahead to prevent these kinds of problems, we continue to assert that it's only a matter of time before an advocate gets sued.

Let's try to extend that clean track record as long as possible.

Legal Needs for Advocates

(A disclaimer here: The following is intended to be an overview of possible needs. Not all advocates will need all these forms of assistance, and there may be other forms of assistance you will need for the advocacy practice you create.)

Some who hope to launch advocacy practices wonder whether they really need a lawyer, or whether they can just start their practice by going online and filling out legal forms.

There is no one-size-fits-all answer to that question. You'll need to assess your own level of self-confidence and tolerance for risk; the self-confidence of developing, reading, and understanding contracts and forms vs fear of the risk of being sued, or losing all your money to legal mistakes.

But even then, you might be a do-it-yourselfer who never runs into a problem that needs a legal bail-out – or it's entirely possible you could hire a lawyer to help you, then be sued and lose everything anyway.

Regardless of whether you decide to hire a lawyer, or handle legal instruments and decisions yourself, you'll want to understand the basics, so that's what you'll find here.

Business Formation

The first legal decision to make as you establish your practice will be to choose your business formation. We looked at an overview of the many types of business entities, like sole practitioners and LLCs in Chapter Six. There are pros and cons to each form, as they regard the risk of losing your investment, or your tax liability, or even your ability to sell your business when you're ready to bow out. There are also differences in meaning from state to state or province to province, further reflected in the paperwork requirements for committing to the type of formation you choose.

You can try to figure it out on your own, or you can invest a few hundred dollars in meeting with a lawyer and having him or her make a recommendation to you. The benefit to meeting with a lawyer at this stage is that you can establish a relationship with one during the good times. Then, if a bad time evolves, you'll have someone to call.

My only real advice about which business entity you should form is to make a decision with an eye on your future. Don't choose your business formation based on today, or even next year. Base it on the long term health of your business, and your exit strategy, too.

Managing Expectations

Anyone who has read much of my writing, or who has heard me speak, knows that I often focus on the concept of managing expectations. I believe that concept is at the heart of all good communication, and that successful management of someone else's expectations will lead to a successful relationship. That's true whether we're talking about a marriage, raising children, workplace relationships – or a professional's relationship with a client or fellow professional, or even an advocate's relationship with a client.

When you bought this book, you did so because you hoped it would provide you with a solid understanding of the basics of starting your health advocacy business. That's what it says on the cover, that's the thrust of each chapter title, and that's exactly what your takeaway has been so far. It was a promise made, and has been a promise delivered.

You didn't buy this book to help you open a hair salon, nor a pizza shop. You also didn't buy it if you've been running a successful advocacy practice for ten years (unless you're just checking out what I might be telling your potential competition!) You didn't buy it to decorate your living room, or to use as a door stop. Why? Because based on the book's description, Index and Table of Contents, you didn't expect those needs would be satisfied by purchasing this book.

In order for me to know how to write this book to be useful to you, and to manage your expectations, thus encouraging you to buy it, I needed a clear idea of what you expected to find in this book.

But just as important as knowing what you would expect to find, was knowing what you would expect that I would not deliver.

For example, you may have hoped the book would tell you exactly how much to charge for your services... but it doesn't. Are you disappointed? Perhaps. However, as you think about it, no where did I provide you with the expectation that the book would give you that information. And what you did learn, in Chapter Seven, was how to figure out how much to charge and how to charge it. So, you may have been disappointed that it wasn't an easy, set-in-stone answer. But the topic was addressed, and a more robust and useful answer was delivered.

As a business owner, you'll need to take the same approach to your clients' needs and expectations and your services, too. We'll look at the client/customer service reasons for that in Chapter Thirteen, but in this chapter we'll look at the legal reasons you need to be diligent about managing expectations. Done right, it will keep you out of legal hot water.

Let's look back at the story about Jason from Bust Those Bills Medical Billing Reviewers. What a nice boon to his business it was for Jason to have the opportunity to appear in a TV interview. He could talk about his business, come across as trustworthy, help people understand the benefits of working with him... great PR. Great promotion.

But what Jason didn't understand was the fine art of managing expectations. Somehow that new client got the impression that Jason was going to save him $50,000 or more on his hospital bill. Now, it's doubtful Jason ever said that. And it's doubtful Jason made any sort of statement that could be reasonably construed to mean that. The problem is, it was heard by someone who wasn't listening reasonably. It was heard by someone who was desperate and wanted to hear it in his own way... and now he's taking steps to make Jason just as miserable as he is.

What Jason needed was a disclaimer.

Disclaimers

Part of successfully managing someone's expectations is making sure they understand what CAN'T be done, as well as what CAN be done, through the use of disclaimers.

By definition, a disclaimer is a statement that tells us there might be an exception to whatever it is we are describing or promising. It's a recognition that no contract can make every possible declaration of what will happen, because an exception may be required based on circumstances outside the contractor's control.

For example: Look at the first paragraph in the section a few pages ago called "Legal Needs for Advocates." I began with a disclaimer, because I recognize that my statements here may not be true for every advocate's circumstances. You live in more than 60 states or provinces, you practice more than a dozen types of advocacy, and we can't begin to count the hundreds of circumstances your clients will present to you.

So let's look at Jason's situation... Jason might have successfully managed that client's expectations is a number of ways, through disclaimers, at various steps in the relationship. During the TV interview, he might have stated clearly how everyone's hospital bill is different, how unusual it was to be able to save a client so much money, that his average savings are no more than a few thousand dollars.... Or he might have not mentioned that example at all since it wasn't really representative. Further, during pre-contract conversations with the client, he might have mentioned over and over again that he could make no guarantees about how much could be chopped from the bill.

And most importantly – and since this is our chapter on legal issues – Jason needed to have a clause in his client contract that stated clearly that no promises were being made about saving specific amounts of money. He could have added a disclaimer to his contract that would have made it clear that no savings were guaranteed. He could have required the client put his initials next to that statement. The client would have signed that contract before Jason started his work. So, had Jason included any of those things, the client would have had no standing to his claim that he thought Jason was promising him a savings of $50,000.

Contracts

I've put the disclaimer horse before the contract cart here, but I've actually done that on purpose. There are many new advocates who begin their work with individuals, whether it's for pay or not, who do so with no contract, no agreement in place. They make the assumption (uh-huh – you know what they say about assuming anything) that because they are being so nice and helpful, the person they are helping will be just the same.

But I'll remind you that few people hire a health advocate because life is going along well or because they are feeling healthy and confident. With the exception of doulas or other forms of birthing advocate and coaches, health advocates are hired because something has gone wrong with either their health or their money or both. Patients or caregivers aren't happy when they hire someone to help them – remember FUD? And when they find someone they trust to hire, they may be so relieved that they develop expectations that are impossible to deliver.

Enter contracts.

Contracts between you and the person you are working for – the client – are intended to spell out exactly what can be expected and must be adhered to, by both parties. When signatures are affixed, then both parties should be able to return to that contract at any time and figure out what needs to be done, what wasn't done yet, or what was done incorrectly.

The first contract you'll need will be an agreement to your scope of work, as we reviewed in Chapter Eight. That contract will be between you and your client, remembering that the client is the person who is writing you the check, and not necessarily the patient, the person you'll be attending to.

If you've hired a lawyer, your lawyer may have a basic work agreement you can modify to fit your advocacy work – with his or her review, of course.

Here are some client contract basics to consider if you are a solo practitioner.

- ♦ List the services you will perform including a list of deliverables (e.g. number of meetings, descriptions of tasks, reports that will be issued or anything else that can be identified).

- ♦ The timing for when they will be performed (with beginning and end dates, or a specified number of hours).

- ♦ How you'll handle extra work should the scope expand.

- ♦ Any limitations to the work. For example, lonely clients may call you several times a day, or expect you to visit them repeatedly. You may want to limit the number of visits, or calls, or whatever other over-use they will subject you to.

- ♦ How much you will be paid, and the payment terms, including what will happen if they don't pay you on time.

- ♦ How any out-of-pocket expenses will be covered. There will be some things you pay for as the ordinary cost of doing business. But others should be reimbursable. Out-of-pocket expenses may include such things as mileage, long distance charges, reimbursements for such things as making copies or picking up a drug prescription. You won't want to charge extra for all those things. Just be sure to distinguish them in your contract.

- ♦ Acceptable reasons for, and a way each party can cancel the contract (30 day notice, in writing, or similar).

- ♦ A statement about any work performed by subcontractors, with limitations (more on this later in this chapter).

- ♦ A confidentiality statement about the terms of the contract.

- ♦ A statement that allows you to terminate the contract in case your client seems to be sabotaging your efforts to do what you were hired to do. For example, an adult son hires you to make sure his mother is taking all her medication, but she flushes it down the toilet. Or, you find out you've been hired to do something that's impossible to do because the client withheld information from you at the outset.

- ♦ I also suggest you add statements to your contract that the client must acknowledge in some way (initials, or checkmarks), such as the fact that you will not be delivering any medical care, that you will not provide transportation, that you cannot guarantee you'll be able to save them any money, or whatever would be appropriate to your advocacy. Remember, you are trying to manage their expectations as well as put a legal agreement into place. Even if such statements would not be considered legally acceptable (which is possible in some states or provinces), at least they would have a statement of expectation that had been called out for them, and you could show intent to be sure their expectations were not unrealistic.

  A list of what those statements might include can be found in the Best Practices, Chapter Thirteen.

It should go without saying that you don't begin your work until the contracts are signed. And, as we learned in Chapter Seven, you need to collect your first payment before you begin your work, too. While all this may sound a bit hardened and harsh, it's professional, and no client should be surprised at either requirement. Might as well get started on the right foot.

Remember Laurie, who tried to help a group of siblings make decisions on behalf of their mother? If she has a contract with that list of "must haves" in place, it will help them figure out who is owed what regardless of the brother's rant.

Put It in Writing

Once you begin your work with a client or patient-client, there may be other situations that come up that require tweaks to your working relationship. As you adjust the relationship, you are not required to update and sign a new contract. Just make sure that you capture any adjustments to your agreement in writing.

For example, maybe your client begins to phone you every day because he is lonely. You learn that all he really wants to do is chat with someone, but he uses your work with him as an excuse to place the call. You know he doesn't realize his time will be on the clock – but how do you make him aware that will be true?

You might tell him.

> *Mr. Miller, I enjoy our chats each day, but please remember that you're paying me for the time I'm working with you. That includes our phone calls, too. So let's be sure we cover the important points right away so that it doesn't get too expensive for you.*

Then follow that up with an email or a letter which requires his signature. Be sure the person who actually signed your original contract is included, if that is someone different from Mr. Miller (such as his wife, son or daughter.) Should any questions arise later about how much money you are owed, you'll have your written notification to use as evidence that Mr. Miller understood about the extra time he was using.

Legal Considerations for Working with Subcontractors

Since we're focused on the subject of contracts, let's take a look at the possibility of bringing in subcontractors, since it's just as important you have an ironclad agreement in place with them, too.

One way to grow your business, and particularly if you are in the early stages when your workload begins to grow but isn't enough for a full time employee yet, then you may want to subcontract some of your work to another person who has the skills and the availability to help you out. You might also want to hire a contractor to help you fulfill some of the services a client needs that aren't really your area of expertise.

(If you'd like a quick refresher on the use of subcontractors, or independent contractors, find the sidebar in Chapter Four.)

So picture this: you have extra work, more than you can handle, and you identify a subcontractor to help you out, then you assign her to one of your clients.

How does your client view that? What preparation have you provided to the subcontractor? What potential hurdles do we have in this new relationship?

Aha – yes! We need to manage expectations.

From the client's point of view, our expectation management won't really be legal in nature, although you might add a clause to your client contract that mentions that you, or someone else, will be providing services. More likely we'll need to manage expectations for our clients with a customer service point of view – so we've addressed that in Chapter Thirteen.

Now let's suppose our new subcontractor enjoys working with our client, and the client is thrilled by the relationship. That's great, right? Well, it is, as long as that client can't shanghai your contractor – talking her into working directly for the client with no middle-person (you!)

Or look at it the other way – suppose your subcontractor decides to tell you the project with Mr. Thomas is completed, and you get paid, but behind your back, your subcontractor begins working directly for Mr. Thomas, cutting you out.

How to prevent either scenario? Of course – build in expectations to both contracts: the client's and the subcontractor's.

In addition, there are many other aspects to a contract between you and your subcontractor. Aspects like:

- Describing the independent contractor status (to make it clear this person is not an employee).
- Listing the services the subcontractor will perform.
- Detailing how much will be paid to the contractor, and the terms (when, how and how frequently).
- Who is responsible for out-of-pocket expenses? Decide between the two of you who will pay for gas, or office supplies, or ink cartridges for the subcontractor's printer. (The answer is usually that the contractor pays for all those, but there could be exceptions.)
- Deliverables: what kinds of reporting do you expect, and how frequently?
- Confidentiality: you both agree to keep the terms of your agreement to yourselves.
- Confidentiality: of patient information.
- What happens if you don't pay on time – mediation? Court?
- The terms under which either of you can sever the relationship.
- Insurance – declaring who is responsible for maintaining insurance (it's usually the subcontractor).
- And – to be sure no one steals your clients – a non-compete clause. This clause usually spells out a period of time that the contractor may not independently contract with anyone they worked with through you, and what happens if they do. (This is what keeps your relationship with Mr. Thomas.

There may be additional clauses to add to an independent contractor's agreement. Consult your attorney if you decide you want to begin adding subcontractors to your team.

Those are only two of the contracts that might be useful to you – one for working with clients, and one for working with subcontractors. Over time you might find others would come into play. Feel free to draw up any sort of agreement you'd like and ask for signatures. That's not to say that anything you put into an agreement will be legal! But it will manage expectations – and that's one of your major goals.

HIPAA / Privacy Concerns

Anyone who has worked in healthcare in the United States since 1996 knows about HIPAA. But for a law that is so well recognized there are very few who really understand it, or what to do about it.

HIPAA (which many people think is spelled HIPPA, and which is pronounced "hip-pah") is the Health Insurance Portability and Accountability Act. Ironically, most of us have no idea how it relates to insurance or portability or accountability, for that matter. What we do know is that it says something about PRIVACY.

The privacy aspects of HIPAA address the sharing and storage of medical records by "covered entities." Covered entities are doctors, hospitals and any company that works on electronic storage or transport of medical records.

Note, no specific mention of health advocates.

But the INTENT of the law might be to cover us. It's just that we are so new, that as of the publication of this book, there is no ruling on whether we are consider covered entities or not.

For our clients' purposes, it doesn't really matter what our legal status is regarding HIPAA. We can, and should behave as if we are covered entities, working hard to protect our clients' privacy. In fact, I would make it very clear to clients and patients that you will treat their records with utmost respect, and will take deliberate steps to keep their records private and secure. But know you'll be doing this as a client service/marketing exercise – as a benefit to your work – and not because you have a legal obligation to do so (yet.)

Of course, the obligation question raises the ugly-to-advocates side of HIPAA. That is, that sometimes providers will be unwilling to share our clients' records with us, and they invoke HIPAA as the reason those records can't be shared.

But they are wrong. As long as you have the proper signatures in place, and a copy of the signature form to turn over to the doctor and his or her staff, then you certainly do have a legal right to gain access to your clients' records.

Here is an excerpt from the US Department of Health and Human Services (HHS) website, addressing consumers[14]:

Who Can Look at and Receive Your Health Information

"The Privacy Rule sets rules and limits on who can look at and receive your health information. To make sure that your health information is protected in a way that does not interfere with your health care, your information can be used and shared...

With your family, relatives, friends, or others you identify who are involved with your health care or your health care bills, unless you object...."

As you can see, the law says your client must object – not provide permission. Certainly, when your client signs a HIPAA permission form, he has not objected.

---

14 http://www.hhs.gov/ocr/privacy/hipaa/understanding/consumers/index.html

Further, in the section written for "covered entities" – the people you'll need to make the requests from, HHS states[15]:

> *A covered entity may use and disclose protected health information for its own treatment, payment, and health care operations activities... Health care operations are any of the following activities: (a) quality assessment and improvement activities, including case management and care coordination;*

So yes – that's you, the advocate, providing case management and care coordination. If any provider tries to get in your way, then invoke the website links provided here to show them that you are well within your client's rights to receive his or her records, or to make appointments, or attend appointments on his behalf or with him (if that's part of your service.)

Another question frequently asked about privacy regards the sharing of information through the Internet. Is it OK to email a client or send them contracts, copies of their records or other attachments?

Until (or IF) there is a ruling that says we are covered entities, there is nothing illegal about sharing information through email. However, if you want to make sure you showcase how serious you are about records security and privacy, you might use one of the several email encryption programs that are available. I've highlighted a few in the Resources in the back of this book.

Client Records and Storage

So now we understand that records need to be kept private, but for how long? Again – because we are new, there are no hard and fast rules.

In 2011, we took a poll of advocates and the majority felt that five years was a good amount of time to store a client's records. The runner-up was 10 years. No consensus.

Is There Such a Thing as Advocacy Malpractice?

If you look up the term malpractice in a dictionary, you learn that it refers to the failure by a professional to perform a task in the manner in which it is expected resulting in injury, loss or damage. Some definitions further qualify the definition by saying that the professional needs to be licensed or certified to conduct that task to begin with.

As advocates, we aren't licensed or certified (see the sidebar in Chapter Five) but we are professionals, and yes, someday I expect an advocate will be sued for malpractice.

Preventing malpractice, no matter what it's called, is why we use airtight legal contracts, and why we have insurance.

---

15 Find a link to access to the entire statement and all consumer and provider information about HIPAA in the Resources section in the back of this book.

Within the medical profession, states and provinces dictate how long records must be kept. The requirements range from six to 10 years, depending on other circumstances such as an ongoing relationship with a patient or work with a pediatric patient (Children's records must be kept until age 18, sometimes longer.)

So for now, the answer is – do what makes sense for you. Five years seems like a fair amount of time, but if 10 years makes you more comfortable, do that. You might even vary the amount of time depending on the client. If a client has died, then keeping them a few years longer will be plenty. But an ongoing relationship may mean you keep records longer.

Since much, if not all of the record keeping you'll be doing will be digital, you can always store them on an external hard drive which will then allow you to remove them from your computer, especially if you take your computer with you to meetings. That's a good way to protect them in case your laptop gets stolen.

For privacy sake, you may want to consider a security password for logging on to your computer. They are easy to set up, and having one may be the difference between just having to buy a new computer if yours is stolen vs. having to own up to the security breach to your client.

It's also a good practice to remove any records from your computer (or any device connected to the Internet), once you are no longer working with that client. Copy the files to an external hard drive, and make a back-up in a second location in case your external media gets too old (remember floppy disks?) or becomes corrupted.

Now that we've taken a look at some of the many ways you can keep yourself on the straight and narrow with the legal system, we still owe it to ourselves to ask – so what if something pops up we haven't anticipated? Just like Melanie Murphy was blindsided by Marvin Malone's family (see the story at the beginning of this chapter) – how do we protect ourselves from the unexpected?

The Dance of Insurance and the Law

In our last chapter, we looked at one kind of dance – a marketing dance. If I had to describe a dance format for marketing, I'd call it a salsa.

There's a dance that takes place between insurance and the law, too. It's more like a tango, as they twine around each other in an attempt to keep harmony in your business. In fact, the law and insurance are so closely woven, that often the questions we think are legal questions instead relate to insurance, and vice versa.

Insurance is based on risk. When you find an insurer who is willing to cover you, they are taking a risk that you are doing everything legally, and that your work isn't too risky. This is one of the main reasons we recommend to advocates that they make it very clear to their clients that they will not perform any medical services – because advocates are not covered, or insured for medical mistakes, or even the perception by a client that a mistake has occurred.

In each aspect of your practice that poses a risk, you'll want insurance to protect you in case some problem crops up that threatens your livelihood, your assets, your life, or all three.

What Insurance Does a Health Advocate Need?

There are several kinds of insurance advocates need, some of which relate to advocacy as a profession, others which relate to being in business, and a few personal insurances to consider.

Insurance is very much affected by the state or province you live in. Provided here is general information about the types of insurances you'll need, but in all cases, you'll need to contact a broker in your state or province who can provide the particulars. Or if you are a member of APHA, you'll find the Insurance Advisor to be very savvy about the insurance advocates need based on where they live and work.

Advocate's Work Insurance

This is the big one, the one most advocates ask about. It's the insurance that addresses your real work. That is: **Errors and Omissions Insurance (commonly called E&O).**

E&O is the insurance that says if you make a mistake, or fail to do something or say something you should have said or done, or if your client just *thinks* you should have said or done something, you will have insurance to back you up and pay for any damages that resulted from the E or the O. This is the insurance that Melanie Murphy would have relied on when she was sued by Mr. Malone's family even though she had done nothing wrong and wasn't even present when Mr. Malone fell.

Because health advocacy is such a new profession, and in particular because there is no nationally recognized certification, nor any state or province that provides licensing, E&O insurance is quite expensive. As of 2012, it runs about $1,500 per year. In order to qualify for it, you have to show what business formation you've chosen, and share the contracts you use with the insurance company because they want to be sure you're covering yourself legally, diminishing your risk.

There are only two or three companies in the United States that will insure advocates for E&O. APHA maintains information about these companies and stays updated on changes.

There are other E&O insurances available for nurses and case managers that are less expensive. But so far, all the policies our experts have reviewed have intentionally excluded coverage for the services most advocates provide.

E&O Insurance is not a place to skimp. Think of it this way: the cost of insurance is about equal to the revenue you'll earn from one client each year. You can't afford to yield your livelihood or your financial stability to someone who has whacky ideas based on misperceptions or unmanaged expectations, merely for the amount of money you earn from one client.

Business Insurances

Property and casualty Insurance: This is the insurance that covers your business property, like your computers, your furniture and other equipment. It will also cover any liability if someone is injured while doing business with you on your property or in your office (although – important – it does not cover liability from errors or omissions while performing your advocacy work.) It will cover problems like losses from crime or a disaster (think earthquake, hurricane or tornado) including business interruption (you can work because your office has been destroyed.) This insurance is called a **Business Owner's Policy, and is known as BOP insurance**.

Included in BOP insurance may be a "non-owned automobile" rider which means that if something happens while you, the personal owner of your car, are driving, your business is

---

Are You a Licensed Professional?

Many people who choose private, independent advocacy are already licensed. Doctors, nurses, nurse practitioners, social workers, lawyers and other licensed medical professionals find advocacy to be the one profession where they can truly help people the way they want to help them.

If you hold a license in one of these medical professions, you may find there are lines drawn between what your license allows you to do, what your insurance allows you to do, and what your work as an advocate should be.

For example, your license may mean you have to limit your geography, and offer your services only within the state or province you are licensed in. If you are a nurse or physician, then you may be qualified to give medical advice, but your advocate insurance may prohibit that. You'll be tempted, but you'll be crossing a line.

The answers to whether these concerns apply to you change with each person's circumstances. They vary by license, by state or province, by insurance policy and by the list of services you hope to offer as an advocate.

So ask! Your attorney and insurer, together, should be able to arrive at the best advice for you.

protected from liability. It's not truly automobile insurance; it's a barrier between your company and the liability of using your personal automobile while you are working. It won't cover any actual damage or injury that result from an accident, but it will put a barrier between use of your personal car, and your business should you be driving your personal car for work-related purposes.

This type of insurance will be relatively inexpensive, depending on exactly what you're covering. If you work from home, it's a rider you add to your homeowner's policy and will add only a hundred dollars or so a year to your premium. Premiums go up from there for office locations (like renter's insurance) and, of course, if you own your own building.

Auto Insurance: if you drive your car for business purposes, you'll want to alert your auto insurance broker. For example, you may drive to client meetings, or to the hospital to provide bedside services, or to Staples to buy a pen. As long as you drive only yourself and not your client, then your auto insurance premiums won't be much higher (if at all) unless you begin driving many more miles than you used to because of your new advocacy work.

This auto insurance is the insurance that covers accidents or damage, unlike the non-owned automobile rider mentioned in the section about BOP insurance.

Driving with clients in your car is another story all together. Transporting clients raises all kinds of potential risk and liability (and insurance costs); so much so, that I recommend you just not do it at all.

In some states and provinces you won't legally be able to transport clients unless you get a livery license (like a cab driver.) In all states and cases, the risk you take just is not worth the potential problems, like an accident, or a client's hand getting slammed in the car door, or getting sick in your car – remember – if it can go wrong, it will go wrong.

If you decide to ignore my don't-drive-your-clients advice (you won't be the first), then be sure you explain to your auto insurance broker exactly what it is you are doing. Then decide from there.

If you decide to adhere to my advice, and a client wants you to drive her to a doctor appointment, explain that you aren't insured to do that, but that you'd be happy to make arrangements for her. Then phone one of the medical transport companies that exist in most locations.

Personal Insurances

If you will be an advocate in practice in the United States, then you must consider health insurance as a "must". Since you will be self-employed, you will no longer be receiving it as a benefit from another employer. If your spouse or domestic partner can cover you with his or her health insurance, then that's a great resource! But other than that, you'll have to find it on your own.

Of course, the resources and landscape of personal health insurance are shifting rapidly through implementation of healthcare reform (Patient Protection and Affordable Care Act.) If you don't have a known and ready-resource for health insurance, then there are a few places to begin asking questions: Your local SBA, SCORE or SBDC office, a Chamber of Commerce or other business-focused organization, members of any business networking organizations (known by names like BNI or tip club.)

One other insurance to mention is **disability insurance**. In effect, disability insurance provides a paycheck if some sort of accident or medical situation renders you unable to work.

When you were employed by someone else, you probably had disability insurance; you may not have even realized it. If something dire happened to you, after a certain period of time, your disability payments would have kicked in, and you would have had the money you need for your mortgage.

As a self-employed advocate, you still run the risk of being disabled, but you no longer have an employer to subsidize the cost of disability insurance. It's worth asking your insurance broker about it, then weighing the risk against the cost.

Insurance is one of those things that you may never need to tap into; it will be good news if you don't. But having it will help you sleep at night, and will keep your business tango with the law and liability from tripping over each other, then falling on the floor.

Sure! Go ahead!
This is a blank page, and it's
your book, so make some notes...

Chapter Eleven
Managing Workflow:
Taking Care of Business

What does "being in business" really look like?

Unless you've been self-employed before, it probably won't look like what you expect.

You may remember the discussion of billable hours. Those are the hours spent working with your client, or on behalf of your client – the work you've pictured as you've contemplated your career as an advocate.

Managing your workflow is process you use to organize and handle the business details that get your client from point A to point B – not necessarily the advocacy work itself, but everything else that supports your work and your clients.

What sorts of details will you need to manage, and what kinds of business questions will your clients have? What forms and contracts will you need? What records will you want to keep? What happens first, then next, then next? How will you most efficiently and effectively deliver your services while growing your practice?

The management devils are in the details and when it comes to people's health and finances, you can't afford to mess with those devils. Can't afford it on their behalf – and can't afford it for your practice either.

What's Workflow?

Workflow is the process by which your product or service is delivered. The process is an organizational management system laid out in a chronological priority system that utilizes specific protocols for effective and efficient management of the enterprise.

Say, what? That all sounds so very business-esque, doesn't it?

So let's break it down.

Your work with almost every client will consist of the exact same business steps:

Steps if You Provide a Paid Assessment	Steps if You Provide a Free Assessment
1. Engagement	1. Engagement
2. First invoice / payment for Assessment	2. Free Assessment
3. Development and delivery of the Assessment (Care Plan)	3. Contract and invoice
4. Contract and second invoice	4. Development and delivery of Care Plan
5. Privacy and records signatures	5. Privacy and records signatures
6. Advocacy / Service Performance	6. Advocacy / Service Performance
7. Review and Evaluation	7. Review and Evaluation
8. Records Delivery, Storage and Endorsement Request	8. Records Delivery, Storage and Endorsement Request
9. Follow Up	9. Follow Up

Of course, once in a while you'll skip one or another of these steps with a client, but for the most part, each one will go from Step 1 to 2 to 3 and so forth.

Each step is an important part of your overall client-management system. The system was developed based on what work we know each client will require from beginning to end. The steps are chronological – obviously you have to engage a client before you do anything else. Obviously you won't ask for an endorsement until your work is done, etc. Priorities determine the placement of some of the steps; in particular, we want to be sure we get paid before we do the work, for example. And each step is comprised of specific forms and protocols to help make sure it's accomplished and complete.

Voila! A health advocate's workflow.

When it's laid out in steps like this, it doesn't seem quite so overwhelming.

When you first get started, going from step to step will seem to take much longer than it should – a little like the new cashier at the supermarket who begins checking people out for the first time. Early in her cashier career, she's painfully slow and you give serious consideration to jumping to another line. After a while she gets much faster (and puts all the heavy stuff at the bottom of the bag, instead of all the heavy stuff into one bag....)

Eventually you'll get to the point where these steps seem like second nature. You'll develop forms and formats – protocols - to use to make it easier on yourself and to remind you of points you have a tendency to forget. You might even add steps on your own to help you manage your workflow.

Let's look more closely at each step now, to determine what each requires to make it work, with a few cautions thrown in, and some examples to make sure they are clear.

Note: The steps are similar for both work processes, but are ordered a little differently due to the extra contract and invoicing step in the Paid Assessment process. The following steps are numbered according to the "Steps if You Provide a Free Assessment".

1. Engagement (convincing them to work with you)

Engagement, meaning getting a client to say "yes"– then signing a contract, too - usually begins with your marketing in general (speaking to groups, your website, your brochures, your business cards, your health expo sponsorship and others), probably focused on a group of people, and eventually boils down to a conversation with one person face-to-face, on the phone, or in rare cases, through email.

It may take only minutes or days – or it may take months or years.

Meeting face-to-face early in the engagement process may be necessary for some patients. One of the most important reasons they seek help from an advocate is because they feel like there has been an empathy disconnect. Either their doctors aren't coordinating their care, or they feel as if the doctor isn't listening – whatever the reason, they crave (and will pay for) face time with a human being who will listen, empathize – and act. That's you.

But most engagements will more likely take place on the phone – so that's what we're going to deal with here. You can add or subtract from this protocol for a face-to-face meeting, or even an email engagement.

The phone rings – how do you answer it? You want to be friendly, but professional. You might answer with your company name, then your name. "ABC Advocates. This is Jennifer. May I help you?" Using a simple "hello" isn't professional enough – sounds like you're at home reading a good book or washing the kitchen floor.

(Since my phone doubles as my home phone and my work phone (for three different businesses!), I usually answer with "This is Trisha." Short, sweet, professional.)

OK – you've got a live one on the phone. Now what?

When you first begin having engagement phone conversations, you probably won't be very good at it. But there will be clues each time for how you can improve the next time. Take notes – whatever seems important. Did the person on the phone balk when you gave him a piece of information? Did he or she sound excited, or relieved, during another part of the conversation?

After your second and third phone conversations, begin to compare your notes. Are they asking for services you don't offer? Consider offering them, or finding someone to partner with who can offer them. Are they located too far away? Do they all claim poverty? (Even the rich ones will claim your services are too expensive for all the reasons we already discussed in Chapter Eight.)

If you're really struggling to get someone to say "yes" then it may be because you're giving away too much information on the phone. Or, as Momma used to say, "Why should they buy the cow if they can get the milk for free?"

Most advocates have big hearts. When someone sounds scared or desperate, we want to help them in any way we can. But if we help them too much, then why would they hire us?

So develop a phone protocol. Ask questions for the first 10 minutes or so, and then, if you feel like this is someone you can help, politely say, "Mr. Burnham, I believe I can help you with this. Let me tell you how I work." Then explain that you'll do an assessment of his needs, or that you charge $xx for XX hours – whatever it is.

If Mr. Burnham keeps asking questions, then answer them generically with something simple like, "Yes, those are services I offer" or "Yes, I think I can help you with that" or "Yes, once we have a contract I can jump in to help you with that."

Remember – you are a business person. You are not a volunteer.

Your "Ask"

The most important part of your phone protocol is called your "ask." It's simply a call-to-action – a question that gets them to say YES. "May I email a copy of the contract to you?" or "How soon would you like to start?"

They may tell you that they can't afford your services. Prepare ahead of time an answer that firmly, but politely tells them that they "can't take it with them"... something like, "I know at the moment that seems like a lot of money. But if you think about it, it's money well spent if it improves the quality or quantity of your life, don't you think?" (See the sidebar on page 117 about Overcoming Objections.)

They may ask you if you are covered by their insurance. If they don't ask, I strongly suggest you bring it up so you know they aren't assuming you do. Then explain to them the reasons outlined in Chapter Eight on why you don't work with insurance, and why it's in their best interest that you don't.

Then, if possible, capture their contact information even if they decide against hiring you. Ask if they are willing to share a phone number or email address. Then, either call or email a week later and ask if they would like to discuss further the idea of your support. (And keep the email address in case you decide to issue an email newsletter in the future.)

What if you don't want to work with a caller? Then let them down gently. You might just price your services way too high. (See page 174 for a way to do this.) Or, just tell them you don't believe you're capable of helping them, but you might be able to refer them to someone else.

2. Assessment (Free or Paid)

Free Assessment

You don't want to spend a lot of time listening to someone's story and needs, then making suggestions or proposals, without knowing that the potential client is likely to engage. Many people would love nothing more than to bend your ear for an hour or more, milk your knowledge bank, and then move on without paying you.

If you insist on providing a free assessment, then you'll still want it to be professional – just not very detailed. Collect enough information about the client's situation, his wants, needs and expectations so you can make an educated guess about the amount of time it will take you to perform the services that need to be performed. Eventually you'll use this information in your care plan (described later in this chapter), so collect as much detail as you want, but you don't have to provide all those details back to a client during a free assessment process.

Then, in proposal form, describe what you've learned and suggest the services that will be required – subject to a full blown assessment. Be sure you don't give away so much information that they don't need to hire you to do the work.

Put your proposal on letterhead (your logo, company name and contact information) so it looks professional, and looks like you have listened carefully. At the end, provide an estimate for the work you'll do. Put your signature on it, and a date they must commit by (within 30 days or 60 days – or one week – that's up to you). Deliver it to the potential client, either by postal mail, email or fax.

Be sure your assessment / proposal is delivered with an Ask, either written or verbal. If they are unwilling to commit right away, then ask again within a day or two. Stay on it until they either commit, or decide against it. Just don't drop the ball on the ask because that's what you'll need to engage your client.

Paid Assessment

Of course, the way to alleviate the problem of not getting paid for your knowledge and help is to provide a paid assessment process. In effect it means that you can spend time with that potential client, draw up a detailed scope of work, and be paid for that portion of your work with them.

If you do decide to go with a paid assessment, then draw up a simple invoice[16] for the amount of the assessment process, and deliver it to the potential client. Once your client has paid you for the assessment it will be time to develop it.

The assessment you'll deliver to a client who has paid you will be far more formal in scope and detail than the one you deliver for free. In effect, you'll be developing a care plan, a road map for defining where the patient is at the moment, where it is he needs to be, and how and when he'll get there. A better description of the care plan can be found later in this chapter.

(Don't forget the pricing idea about subtracting the cost of the assessment from the eventual contract you draw up. See page 97.)

3. The Contract

There's no better feeling than the one you get when the first person says "yes!" But it's an even better feeling once you have a signature.

Contracts, of course, are the domain of lawyers and yes – you do need a lawyer to create a contract for your use[17]. The important elements for the contract are listed in Chapter Ten.

Of course, if you meet your new client in person, then you can have printed copies of your contract for signing (take at least two – one for the client and one for you.)

But if you come to verbal agreement on the phone or through email, you'll need to have easy ways to accept signatures from your new client. You can always attach it to an email, ask them to sign it and postal mail, email or fax it back to you.

Or, you might make use of the one of the online document applications available that allow for secure signature exchange. Find a list of these applications in the Resources in the back of this book.

Invoicing and Collection

Asking for money. If there is one thing that all new advocates tell me they really hate doing, it's just that – asking someone to pay them.

Here's the bad news. Everyone who was ever a successful private health advocate had a dreaded "first time" asking for money. You will, too.

Here's the good news. The first time only happens once. (Thank you Captain Obvious!) It's a little easier the second time, and gets even easier with each subsequent request. After a while, it's just part of how you do things, and while I would never tell you it gets to be

---

16   Find a sample invoice in the Resources section in the back of this book.

17   APHA does have sample contracts and other documents that can be used for review with an advocate's attorney. They are available only to members. Find APHA contact information and an offer for a free trial membership in the Resources section in the back of this book.

simple or second nature, I will tell you that it becomes a part of your professional persona. Like filing income taxes – it's not easy and you don't have to like it – but it's doable.

And it's not nearly as complex as you may think. You will have already settled on a price, as per your contract, so it's really just a matter of providing an invoice, then waiting for payment.

The more difficult part may be explaining to your client that services cannot be started until payment has been made. As you do that the first few times, just remember that it's the professional approach to business – and you are a professional.

Just like you will manage your client's expectations about their journey through their healthcare, I will now manage your expectations about asking for, and collecting payment. The more you know and expect, the less daunting and difficult it will seem.

First, a bit of a pep talk here (cue the pom poms):

YOU ARE WORTH EVERY PENNY YOU ASK FOR. And YOU ARE MORE THAN WORTH EVERY PENNY SOMEONE PAYS YOU. You are the person who is going to help someone manage their quality or quantity of life, and their financial stability, too. There is nothing more important to any human being because by performing your advocacy services, you are helping them and their loved ones, too.

OK – pep talk over – back to business....

In Chapter Six we looked at the many ways you can accept payments. Make sure these arrangements have been made ahead of time.

Now go draw up a simple invoice, provide it to your new client, and wait to be paid.

When should you start doing the work – before or after payment? I have very definite ideas on that topic. See Chapter Eight for "When to Ask for Your Money."

4. Development of a Care Plan or Scope of Work

"If you don't know where you are going, you'll wind up someplace else." (Yogi Berra)

I'm not sure Yogi Berra knew much about health advocacy, but he certainly knew how important it is to figure out what you're trying to accomplish.

And so it is true with your work for your clients. In order to get your client from where he is to where he wants or needs to be, you need a plan – a road map to help you figure out where you need to be, and how to get there.

There are a variety of names for such a plan. Some call it a care plan. Some call it a work proposal or scope of work. Maybe you can think of a clever name for your own proposal or planning process. For now, in this book, we'll call it your care plan.

What's Included in a care plan?

(In all cases in this section of Chapter Eleven, when I refer to the client I mean the patient you are working with.)

A care plan will have a number of components, some of which will be for your records only, and some you'll share with your client.

If you provided a free assessment, then it will be a much expanded version of what you have already given the client; not just the "here's what's wrong and we will attempt to fix it," but the "here's how we'll fix it" too.

However, if you have been paid to put together an assessment, then you can use this outline for a care plan, and deliver most of it as your assessment.

Here are some suggested components of a care plan:

- Identification of the client and the advocate (you!).
- A situation analysis or current status.
- The challenges your client faces that you are expected to help alleviate
- The client's goals and expectations and a statement of whether or not those goals and expectations can be met.
- For those expectations you will tackle, an outline of what is needed to make them happen.
- Timing issues, such as priority or chronology, dates or deadlines.
- Privacy Statement
- Additional Services

Here is more information on each component of the care plan:

1. Identification: for the parties who are part of the assessment – the client and you. This just needs to be a statement that says, in effect, "this is the client to whom this proposal is being made" and "this is the advocate / service provider who is making the proposal."

2. Situation analysis: Describe the client's current health circumstances as they stand prior to you performing any of your services. "Client was diagnosed by _____(who) based on (list symptoms) and (list tests)". Or "Client has been billed $52,000 by XYZ Hospital." You can make this as detailed as you want to be. Make sure it is detailed enough so your potential client feels as if you have listened carefully. (You may have already provided this, or part of this, if you performed the free assessment.)

3. Challenges: What are the problems your client faces? These are not just the problems they have told you they are having. There may be additional problems you have identified during your assessment process – anything they need help with. Just define what those things are at first – not their solutions. We'll deal with those in a moment.

4. Expectations: What does this client hope you will accomplish? What are his goals, or what does he expect you can do for him? Important here is to acknowledge his requests, but to be clear on whether or not it can be accomplished – that balance with reality. He may be a diabetes patient who is going blind and, in his heart of hearts, wants you to be able to restore his sight. Or maybe he had an emergency appendectomy, has no health insurance, and expects you to convince the hospital to make his bill just disappear. Not going to happen.

However, there are many things you may be able to do for both those unrealistic clients that will serve them well. Just be clear on which are realistic vs which ones are improbable.

5. Tasks and Services to Be Provided:

Here is where you will outline or describe how you'll accomplish those goals and expectations you listed in #4. "Advocate will stay by Mr. Fredericks' bedside during his stay at XYZ Hospital." Or "Advocate will organize all existing bills." Or " Advocate will negotiate with providers to reduce bills as much as possible."

Important note: How detailed this section should be is determined by whether or not you have already signed a contract for execution of these steps. If you put together most of the care plan for the Paid Assessment, but don't yet have a signed contract for executing the steps, then make sure you don't put so much information in the care plan that the client could just take off and do the work on his own.

On the other hand, if you are already under contract, then being able to see the steps described in full will help your client understand why you are worth every penny he is paying you.

This is also a place to show your real value as an expert; that is, list needs your client didn't know she had. For example, if she will undergo chemo, mention finding

What Makes Your Client Tick?

As you work with your potential new client, particularly during the engagement process, but also during the assessment process, there will be specific questions that aren't so much about the person's medical condition, but are more about who he or she is as a person, their belief systems, and what they want for themselves in the long term.

For example, you may learn that there is an underlying fear because his mother died from Alzheimer's and he's having some trouble with his memory. That knowledge will help you work with him differently than if you didn't know he was fearful.

For a client who is already up to his eyeballs in financial problems, there may be no way organizing his bills is ever going to improve his ability to pay them. And maybe he already filed bankruptcy so that even that is not an option. You need to know that.

What about her approach to healthcare? Does she have interest in some of the complementary or alternative approaches like acupuncture or meditation?

Does your client have a religious or spiritual belief system that will impact his or her decision making? That's a good piece of information to know ahead of time. So ask! A client who has a terminal disease and a strong belief in an afterlife may not react the same way to bad news as a client who is agnostic.

There is no one-size-fits-all list of questions to ask. Further, each advocate's list will vary by the types of services they offer.

Keep track of these kinds of questions, and others you find important, too. Develop your own assessment guidelines, but don't be afraid to vary them from client to client, and to update them from time to time, too.

someone to care for her pets on the days she will have treatment, or that you will find transportation arrangements for her. It's entirely possible she never thought of those needs, and she'll feel relieved, and appreciative, that you did.

6. Timing: In any care plan, some steps need to be done before others can be done, or some will take priority of importance over others.

If you will be cleaning up someone's medical bills, then obviously you'll need to organize them first, then decide which ones need to be paid before others, or which ones can be negotiated.

If you will be helping someone who has just been diagnosed with cancer, then you'll want to be sure to get copies of their medical records before you seek a second opinion, or you'll want to be sure the client has a thorough knowledge of all her treatment options before she begins chemo.

7. Privacy Statement: This section is just for reassurance to your client that you will keep your work and plans with your client private. If you have chosen to use encrypted email for information exchanges, that can be mentioned here, too.

8. Additional Services: As a professional, there will be additional services you know your client may decide he needs as he transitions through your care plan, even though he doesn't want them included at the outset. There's no harm in listing them here with brief descriptions, with a statement telling him how they may be added to the care plan later.

You may wish to add other components to your care plan, too, depending on the services needed, or those you provide.

Care Plan Presentation

As you write out each point of the care plan, use action words as much as possible. When your client reads over the plan, he wants to know you are DOING SOMETHING. He wants to know that when you're finished, he will be able to easily recognize the results—that they will be measureable and can be checked off the list.

For example, look at these two statements:

- ♦ Research potential treatments for chronic Foot-in-mouth Disease.

- ♦ Research doctor's recommendations for treatment of chronic Foot-in-mouth Disease, uncover any additional possible treatments, list and describe them to Mr. Thomas in an understandable format.

If you were a client, which one would you appreciate more?

Physical presentation of the care plan to your client is important, too. Not only should it be full of good information, supplied in detail, but it should look the part. Deliver it in a nice folder. Get your logo printed on stickers, then adhere one to the outside of the folder. Inside the folder you can place the care plan, plus a copy of your brochure, maybe some printed articles about being a smart patient, your business card, and more. You may also want to include some of the paperwork you'll need signatures on if you haven't already included them.

Make it look as if it was worth every penny you charged them for it.

5. Privacy and Records Signatures

If you didn't already do so when your contract was signed, this is the time to get your privacy / HIPAA permission form signed. You may use a HIPAA permission form (find access to one in the Resources section in the back of this book) or use your own form. Each of your client's providers will want one, so get several original signatures, if possible.

6. Advocacy / Providing Your Services

At long last! It's time to do what you do best – advocate!

While this is the most important work you do, I'll provide very little input to that process here. After all – I'm the business expert, but you are the advocacy expert. I can't tell you how to do those parts of your job.

I will provide some advice for managing those services though.

When you first begin your work and you have only one or two clients to juggle, it will be fairly easy to keep them straight. You will keep lists of which doctors which client sees, or which bills come in when – whatever it is that needs to be tracked for that one individual patient.

But what happens when you find yourself with a handful of clients, all with different needs, different schedules, different diagnoses or family members all over the country?

That's when it's time to implement some sort of tracking program – a way to organize the myriad details for each client, ranging from the steps listed in this workflow chapter (Did Mr. Logan already sign his contract?) to the many details of their actual care needs. (What is Mrs. Fordham's dermatologist's name?) to appointment or meeting dates, to invoices and payments, and everything in between.

The biggest problems you'll run into are when some of the information overlaps or conflicts. How can you be sure you won't schedule meetings with two clients at the same time in different doctor's offices on opposite sides of town?

You'll want to develop a tracking mechanism that works for you. It may be a series of notebooks in combination with a master calendar. It may be a spreadsheet that you maintain on your computer. Or you may wish to subscribe to one of a handful of tracking software programs that are built with advocates and case managers in mind. (You can find some of these management software packages listed in the Resources to this book.)

If you think you would like to grow your business one day enough to accommodate for subcontractors, or even employees, then look for options for helping them manage the many details of their clients, too, but perhaps without access to the invoicing and collections part of the work. Once you add subcontractors to the mix, your juggling will take on new dimensions. So to the extent you can think about how they, too, will access the tracking mechanism you are using, you'll have less of a problem adding them to your team.

A note about tracking hours: Among the tracking you'll want to do will be tracking the amount of time your work takes you to do, then deciding how much of that is under your control, vs, how much of it is variable according to the client.

For example, assessment time will always be variable by the client because some talk more than others, and some have bigger challenges than others. Some tasks will become easy to quantify because they include time at your computer or driving from place to place.

Tracking your time is important for two reasons. First, because your billing may be based on the time you spent doing the work. Second, because it will be far easier for you to estimate time in the future, for future potential clients, if you have tracked times to accomplish certain kinds of tasks previously.

7. Review and Evaluation

As you approach the end of your work with your client, you'll want to begin planning for your review and evaluation step.

First, you'll want to return to your contract and care plan to be sure everything has been covered. Did you accomplish all you had promised? Did you do even more? Were there steps you didn't accommodate for that you'll just have to "eat" (not bill the client for) because you didn't estimate for them well?

Do your own review and analysis of what, if anything, remains undone. Once you can say "Check! We're finished!" it will be time to have a conversation with your client.

As you review your work with your client, look at it as both an evaluation of the work that has been done, and as a marketing opportunity, too.

You may wish to provide a written evaluation of everything that was accomplished, lessons learned, and what the client should know for the future. Your client may be just amazed at everything you did! Pointing out the extras you did, perhaps accompanied by an "N/C" on an invoice (meaning, "no charge") can be a silent but powerful way to impress your client – who will tell others. Great word-of-mouth.

If you are still owed money, then providing this evaluation step just prior to expecting to be paid for that last invoice can be the great motivator for receiving that last check.

8. Records Delivery, Storage and Endorsement Request

Your work is finished. Your client has what he or she needs, and you've compared your contract to your delivered services to be sure the i's have been dotted and T's are crossed.

Two final details are important just as the current relationship ends.

First, you'll now have many records in your possession that you might decide belong in your client's hands. Once they have paid that final invoice, then any records you think they should have can be delivered to them.

If they are paper records, then it's wise to keep copies of any originals you return to your client. If they are electronic you'll have copies, of course, and you can deliver digital copies on a thumb drive or a CD you burn on your computer, both well-labeled, perhaps with your logo on them, too.

Along with their records, give them some marketing materials to use on your behalf, too. A few of your brochures and business cards is all that's needed. If someone asks them who helped them out, they will have those pieces to give to that someone else – they'll be marketing your services for you.

This is also a great time to ask your client to endorse your work – to provide a testimonial for you. If they are web savvy, you can create a place on your website where they can write one and submit it to you. If they are still part of the pen and paper set, then give them a form to fill out and a stamped, self-addressed envelope. Ask for permission to use their testimonial in your marketing materials. If they prefer to remain private, then ask them to provide you with a pseudonym you can use when you make the endorsement public.

Then use them![18]

9. Follow Up

Sometime in the not-too-distant future (a month, a few months), reach out to your former client again. Remember, you've left behind marketing materials – so that gives you a good excuse to call.

---

18 If you are a Premium member of APHA, then you can add testimonials to your directory listing at AdvoConnection. Learn more in the Resources section in the back of this book.

Ask how they are doing, have they run into any more problems, remember an anecdote from when you worked together, tell them you ran into a mutual friend, or – and this is important when it's appropriate – thank them if they referred someone to you, whether or not you actually engaged with that person to do any work.

Depending on the response you get, you might ask them if they need your services further. Or, ask if they need any more of your business cards to give away.

Touching base lets them know that you still think about them and that your commitment didn't end with the contract.

And if they do refer someone to you who ends up signing a contract and working with you, consider giving them a gift as a thank-you. Maybe a gift card to a local coffee shop or restaurant, or even Amazon.

Develop a Resource Bank

One of the most valuable assets you can create for yourself is a Resource Bank. In fact, that Resource Bank can be valuable enough for you to include in the sale of your business if and when it's ever time to sell it. It can truly add to the valuation of your business.

I'm not talking about just a list of doctors or facilities or transportation providers or wheelchair dealers.

I'm talking about a robust database that includes everything from contact phone and email, to the right person to talk to in a business that can help you, to that persons' nephew's birthday (so many favors get done just because you ask how someone's nephew who has just applied to college is doing). Records on pricing, and customer service – any details you think you might make use of in the future, including information about bad service so that you won't contact an unacceptable resource again.

The more exhaustive your Resource Bank, the less time it will take you to accomplish any tasks that require those resources. You'll no longer need to make a dozen phone calls just to get phone numbers or recommendations. Nor will you have to weed through Google's 468,000 results for "medical transport, Wichita."

Chapter Twelve
The Standards and Ethics of Health Advocacy

A handful of professions give us pause. If you met someone new, and they told you their profession was one of these, you'd stop to wonder what makes them tick.

Used car salespeople

Politicians

Telemarketers

Now – I expect that most of the people who practice these professions are good, upstanding, honest people. But on the whole, as a stereotype, they are listed among the least respected professions. Also included are real estate salespeople, those who work in the sex trade, professional athletes, actors and stockbrokers. [19]

Too many lack scruples, or have little or no integrity.

At first glance, those professions don't seem to have much in common. It's really tough to compare a professional athlete with a used car salesperson or a politician (Jesse Ventura notwithstanding).

But they do have one thing in common and that is, that as each of those professions got its start, there was no set of ethical standards or codes of conduct for them to follow. Even today, most of those professions still have no standards to follow, and those that do don't police themselves. You have to wonder why they list ethical standards at all.

We don't ever want that to happen among private, independent advocates.

I repeat (loudly and boldly)...

We don't ever want that to happen among private, independent health advocates.

---

19 http://voices.washingtonpost.com/thefix/parsing-the-polls/parsing-the-polls-you-like-me.html

And so, one of the most important aspects to getting started as a health advocate is to understand the foundation of ethical standards that support the profession, and the importance of adherence to those ethics, right from the get-go.

The History of Private, Independent, Health Advocacy and Its Professional, Ethical Standards

While it may be difficult to conceive of such a new profession having a "history" – it does.

In fact, the explosion of new advocates choosing to become private, independent advocates comes on the backs and hard work of a handful of individuals who have actually performed this kind of work for more than a decade. Like many of you, the readers of this book, most of those individuals began with personal stories that compelled them to take up advocacy.

Among the early-in advocates was a man named H. Kenneth Schueler. Ken, who spent much of his early career as a consultant for UNICEF, was himself diagnosed with Stage IV Lymphoma in the mid-1990s. Through his own rigorous research, asking the right questions of the professionals, and making choices he felt were right for him (which were not necessarily the recommendations being made to him), Ken was able to pull himself through that lymphoma, and went on to enjoy many more healthy years.

By the late 1990s, Ken realized what it had taken to triumph over his lymphoma. Although he had not worked in a clinical setting, he knew that his ability to find resources had been improved because he did have some background in healthcare. He decided to see if he could make a living helping others navigate their care in some of the same ways he had navigated it himself.

By 2007 and into 2008, as the healthcare system in the United States began to become more and more complicated, and politicians and the news media began to focus more and more on the struggles Americans encountered trying to get the best care for themselves, more people started private advocacy businesses. They began to network among themselves, and in 2009, two organizations, AdvoConnection and the National Association of Health Advocacy Consultants (NAHAC), were launched to facilitate the establishment of the profession.[20]

In 2010, Ken was asked to oversee a committee to establish a Code of Ethics for the profession. NAHAC adopted much of Ken's code, then required its membership to agree to abide by the NAHAC Code beginning in late 2010.

---

20 NAHAC was formed to support the advocacy work itself, in particular the medical-navigational aspects of the profession. AdvoConnection was established to support the business needs of those advocates who wished to start and grow private practices, and does not limit itself to med-nav advocacy only. In 2012, the AdvoConnection membership organization changed its name to the Alliance for Professional Health Advocates (APHA.)

Because NAHAC's membership does not require its members to be independent advocates, nor working in private practice, and because there are also many forms of advocacy that aren't medical-navigational in nature (e.g medical billing advocates, case managers or family mediators), a more generic, but no less stringent code of professional standards was developed in 2012 for the profession at large.

That code, called The Health Advocate's Code of Conduct and Professional Standards was based on Ken Schueler's original, but modified and simplified for clarity.

That Code of Conduct and Professional Standards can be found at www.HealthAdvocateCode.org. All private, independent advocates, as well as others who hope to work into the industry, are invited to subscribe to the code and put its logo on their print materials, websites, and in other places. You do not need to be a member of any advocacy organization to subscribe to the Code and make that public. Subscribing to the Code and sharing the logo are free.

When you are ready to let the public know that you are a practicing private advocate, it's a great idea to log on to the Code website and subscribe.

Ethics, Code of Conduct or Best Practices – What's In a Name?

So there are two approaches to our work as advocates:

1. The foundation for our work is the Code of Conduct and Professional Standards which are built from a strong ethical base. These are client-centered, values-based, rules of conduct that stand behind every other behavior we exhibit or decision we make. They are all about integrity. They are very "golden rule" in nature – the way we treat others is the way we want to be treated ourselves. This code is not optional.

2. The best practices (found in Chapter Thirteen) are the specifics for how the Code of Conduct and Professional Standards is applied to decision making. They are examples of how the Code is implemented. They are more like guidelines, even if some come with some arm-twisting attached (because the lawyers tell us they are that important.)

But don't sweat the differences. Read through the Code here in Chapter Twelve, and the Best Practices in Chapter Thirteen. Then decide how you will embrace them, realizing that their goal is to maximize integrity within our new profession, and showcase your intention of integrity, too.

The Health Advocate's Code of Conduct and Professional Standards

(Dedicated to Ken Schueler and those who have lived these tenets with integrity since the establishment of health advocacy as a profession.)

As a new profession, one that does not yet benefit from a nationally or internationally recognized set of credentials, it is imperative that health advocates adhere to common set of behaviors and standards in order to promote integrity within the profession.

1. Health advocates will practice with compassion and respect for the patients, clients and families with whom they work.

2. Health advocates' primary commitments are to promote the health, safety, and rights of their patients and clients.

3. Health advocates will, at all times, be transparent in their work with clients. They will disclose to clients their credentials, experience, pricing structure, and any financial relationships they hold with other professionals, businesses or institutions.

4. Health advocates will, at all times, maintain privacy on behalf of their patients and clients and will keep confidential all activities and records according to agreements among them, and any applicable laws.

5. Health advocates will guide and assist their clients-patients in medical decision-making but at no time will make decisions about health or medical care or payment for medical services on their behalf.

6. Health advocates will promote use of their client-patients' values and belief systems as the foundation for their decision-making.

7. Health advocates will, at all times, practice within their competency. Any requests for services outside the advocate's expertise will be referred to someone else who is equipped to provide those services to ensure the client-patient is benefitting from the best knowledge base.

8. Health advocates will, at all times, work within their professional boundaries and will reject any requests or demands that would cause them to violate those boundaries. Such violations may include, but are not limited to, accepting money or gifts as compensation for referrals to other professionals, fulfilling requests to perform illegal or unethical actions, developing a romantic or sexual relationship with a client or someone related to the client, agreeing to perform any duties

without the disclosure or input needed from the client, or any other circumstances that could result in conflicts-of-interest or the inability to fully perform the work the two parties have agreed upon.

9. Health advocates will not discriminate. They will at no time refuse to work with someone due to that person's race, religion, culture, gender, or sexual preference.

10. Health advocates will continue to pursue education to further their knowledge base, skill set, and practice in order to provide client-patients with the most current information relevant to his/her health situation.

If you will work from an office, especially one that clients or potential clients will visit, you may want to print this list – even frame them. You can find a downloadable, printable version on the website at: www.HealthAdvocateCode.com

Just subscribe to the Code at that site, and you will be taken to badges and a printed version.

Now let's take a look at the best practices which emanate from these standards.

Sure! Go ahead!
This is a blank page, and it's
your book, so make some notes...

Chapter Thirteen
Best Private Advocacy Business Practices

So we've tackled workflow – from A to Z, soup to nuts – the steps required to get you started in business, then taking a client from needing you, to being happy he hired you.

And we've examined our code of professional standards with its focus on integrity.

I'm sure you've noticed, though, that there are some big gaps. It's quite the leap from "keep track of your resources" to promising not to discriminate or make decisions for your client.

Of course, it would be impossible to cover every scenario for every client who might ever hire you, especially because each advocate provides different services.

Further, health advocacy is so new that to this point, there haven't been any defined expectations yet. With no national certification or licensing, you're just expected to do whatever it makes sense to do.

But there are some generalizations we can make that influence major portions of your work. They may be ways to provide good customer service, or keep you out of legal trouble. They may be tried and true ways to get around the healthcare system, or they may simply be common sense. Most apply specifically to our work as advocates, but some are actually just good business advice.

They are best practices. "Best" - because they are win-win. When we conduct our work according to these practices, then our clients, our practices, and we, as individuals benefit. Good business karma.

In effect, these best practices answer the question, "How can we best serve our clients' needs, professionally, ethically and legally while benefiting and protecting ourselves, too?"

Clients' Needs?

In this case, "need" doesn't address specific services. Instead it addresses clients' emotional and psychological needs – how they behave because of the situation they are in, and what they can expect from the relationship with you.

Here are some of the client needs addressed by our best practices:

Clients need to trust.

If you or a loved one have ever been diagnosed with a difficult ailment or condition, then you know – it feels like the rug has been pulled out from under you. It's like a psyche-earthquake, as if your entire foundation has shifted beneath you. The well-functioning body you've always depended on (which you also probably took for granted) has betrayed you! And like any betrayal, trust evaporates.

YOU, the independent and objective advocate, perhaps above all others, need to be trustworthy at this time. A rock. You need to make promises, follow through, manage expectations, be empathetic and compassionate – all that. You need to do it because that's the kind of person you are, because you have integrity, and because that's what you're being paid to do.

Clients need to know what will happen as a result of choices they make.

A client's decision must be based on a solid situation analysis, plus a solid understanding of the consequences of the decisions they make, including the consequences of not making a decision. This comes under the title of "managing their expectations." So whether you're dealing with a health matter, or an argument among family members, you'll need to be clear about what the potential outcomes or consequences will be.

Clients need to feel as if they are in control.

Remember the FUD theory we discussed in Chapter Nine? FUD = Fear, Uncertainty and Doubt and there's no question, whether your client is the patient, or a family member, or even an employer – the reason you've been hired is to satisfy that FUD.

That said, the reason they are so fearful, uncertain and doubtful is because they feel so very vulnerable – so totally out of control of their medical or financial situation.

To the extent you can do it, you want to return some of that control to their hands, and some of our best practices are intended to do just that.

Clients need to separate business from personal.

Since, as an advocate, you will deal with the most personal matters of your client's life – his or her health and money – it is easy for the lines to blur between what's personal and what's business.

Clients may become very dependent on you, and often, dependency breeds familiarity. Yet, as an advocate, you need to be sure it doesn't breed so much familiarity that necessary boundaries are crossed. Circumstances will dictate whether or not there is time for real friendship later, after the business relationship ends. But as long as the business relationship exists, keep the business and personal separate.

Clients need to understand your limits.
Desperate clients, or those who are fearful, uncertain and doubtful, may have expectations of you that you cannot possibly fulfill. Even if they know intellectually that you're not a miracle worker, it doesn't mean they won't have hope in their subconscious that you are an angel sent from above to fix their medical or financial challenges.

One client will expect her advocate to make her cancer go away. Another client will expect that $50,000 hospital bill to evaporate. Still another client will lean on you to enable his father, who lives 1500 miles away, to become independent again.

The difficulty is that these expectations may be unspoken. Sometimes advocates must listen between the lines of the words being used, as opposed to those that go unsaid, but are still expected.

If a client begins to have expectations of you that you can't possibly fulfill, then your relationship is doomed. Your client will be disappointed, and you'll feel as if you have failed, or at least as if you have fallen short. That's lose-lose.

Clients need to understand the consequences of negative behavior.
Unless you've already worked with a handful of clients, this point will seem odd. Negative behavior from a client?

Yes. And in some of the oddest ways. I've heard stories of clients who yelled, or swore, called their advocate names, made impossible demands, made overt sexual passes, and stopped payment on checks. People who, prior to getting sick or hurt, might never have behaved that way, but who somehow, perhaps due to the stress and strife of their new and horrible situation, have developed a sense of entitlement.

Like other needs, this one will be settled by managing your client's expectations. Clients need balance, and it's up to you, as their advocate, to provide it. That's the bottom line.

The best practices listed here are intended to help you impose that balance for your clients.

What About Your Needs?

Sometimes a best practice is more about protecting ourselves.

That protection is mostly legal protection, but it also speaks to our ability to be insured for the work we plan to do. And there's some safety advice thrown in for good measure.

Sometimes clients, perhaps out of desperation, or maybe because they don't know any better, will ask us to do things that we cannot legally, or ethically do. Some of our best practices will help you better understand how to handle those situations.

What to Expect from These Best Practices

Some of our best practices are the result of outside influences. Therefore, we need to remember that they are fluid, and may change over time. For example, we know some will be affected by the advancement of electronic medical records, digital communications and telemedicine, even healthcare reform in the United States.

Best practices will be applied differently from client to client. Your clients' personalities and needs will be a constant challenge and will often dictate which of these best practices you'll need to implement.

In cases where there may be legal questions about how business is handled, the practice suggestion will be based on its legality (if that can be determined), what your insurance will require you to do, and what is in your overall best interests, even if doing something differently would be beneficial to your client.

Are these best practices compulsory? No, they are not. You may choose to embrace or ignore them. You are, afterall, an *independent* health advocate. But know they are put together based on experiences, and anticipated problems, including the school of hard knocks.

Our list of Private Health Advocate Best Practices is never complete; in fact, you might have some to add to this list based on your own experiences over time. If you do, we'd love for you to share them, too! You can find contact information in the back of this book.

Finally, I've listed them here in categories, and each practice is listed only once even though it might easily be included in an additional category.

Customer Service Best Practices

1. Ask how your client would like to be addressed.

Years ago I heard from an 85-year-old woman named Mary who was quite upset that the "child" who called her name while she sat in the doctor's waiting room addressed her as "Mary!" She felt that was disrespectful and preferred to be called Mrs. Johnson.

It makes no difference that the young woman meant no disrespect; it was Mary's perception.

We can take a lesson from Mary's book, however. When you first encounter a potential client, ask what he or she prefers to be called. Simple. Then tell him or her what you prefer to be called, too.

2. Communicate with "all" your clients, but keep your focus on one.

Some clients aren't just one person. Some are comprised of a patient, and a family who surrounds that patient. (That "family" might even be a close friend or partner.) It may be that the patient you are working with isn't really, technically your client if, for example, her adult son is writing the checks.

Based on your patient's and client's mutual agreement, it's good practice to keep in touch with those "extra" clients in the relationship. If you accompany Mom to a doctor appointment, ask her if it's OK for you to contact her son to tell him about what you both learned.

This is particularly important in dealing with the elderly, or a very sick partner, or, more obviously a child.

And, not to be morbid, but it's important that if your patient-client is at risk of dying before your work is finished, and you still need to be paid.

However, while we're discussing inclusion – here's a situation to avoid:

When you are talking to others about your patient-client, and he or she is in the room – be sure you include them in the conversation. Patients report being irked, and sometimes hurt, because an advocate or loved one is present in the exam room, and the doctor begins talking directly to that third party as if the patient isn't even there.

So, yes, it's important to include the important "extras". But it's even more important to keep continual focus on the patient-client you're responsible for.

3. Make regular contact with current clients.

In some client relationships, there will be long periods of time while you're waiting for whatever is next. Maybe the next chemo won't take place for three weeks, or maybe you're waiting on next month's bills to get them organized and managed....

Check in with your client anyway. As long as you still have an active contract, a good rule of thumb would be to contact your client once a week, even if it's only to ask how they are feeling, or whether there's anything new they would like to share.

Of course, if you are juggling a dozen different clients at the same time, you don't want these calls to last for too long – they can eat up hours of time that would not be billable.

You can actually manage the time spent with a little expectation management. Tell your client you'll be checking in once a week, for just a brief call. When you actually make the call, tell him you have just a few minutes, but wanted to check in with him – and then make sure, unless you learn of something huge you need to be involved in, that the call really does last just a few minutes.

4. Listen, listen, listen and be empathetic.

One of the biggest reasons any advocate is hired is because patients don't feel that others who are important to their situation are listening. They feel as if their doctors don't spend enough time with them, or actually hear what they are saying. They are positive that billing clerks or insurance companies aren't listening to reason. Caregivers are sure they are being ignored not just by the loved one they care for, but by the professionals they must refer to for help....

But you, as the advocate, can and should listen, and do so actively. In this case, active listening refers to a give and take that makes it very clear the client is being heard. That active listening should include a hefty dose of empathy, because it's empathy that assures your client you've internalized what he has just told you.

That empathy may be comprised of being surprised, sympathetic, appalled, flabbergasted, gobsmacked, upset, compassionate, dismayed, entertained, horrified, frustrated, outraged, supportive – whatever is appropriate. Followed quickly by reassuring your client that whatever that situation is, you will try to find a way to alleviate it, repair it, or at least improve upon it in some way.

5. Acknowledge, confirm and be empathetic.

As your client explains important information to you, it's important that you acknowledge what you've been told, confirm that you understand it correctly, and when appropriate, react once again with empathy.

Your client, a week after knee surgery, states, "My knee is just killing me!"

Appropriate acknowledgements and confirmations might be,

> *"I'm sorry to hear your knee still hurts." Or*

> *"Does it hurt more or less than it did yesterday? That will help us figure out if it's at least beginning to improve." or*

> *"Is this pain similar to what you've experienced before? Or is it new? Let's figure out if we should check in with the doctor."*

> *"I hate that it still hurts you! The doctor said it would be painful for up to 10 days. Do you still have some of that prescription he wrote for you?"*

In all these cases, your client knows you've heard her, understood what she has told you, that you empathize with her, and that you're thinking about possible next steps. You are providing her with that much needed peace of mind.

6. Make your clients feel as if you are totally focused on them individually.

This is best explained by some Do's and Don'ts.

Do: return phone calls as quickly as possible, be prompt for meetings, and take other steps to be timely and client-centered. Your client should feel as if he or she is your only current concern.

Don't: use excuses that place the blame on other clients, such as "I'm sorry I'm running late – I was with another client." Or "I couldn't call you back today because I was working on a proposal."

When clients are sick, or frustrated, they don't want to think you're "cheating" on them! They want to feel as if your world revolves around them.

Of course, intellectually they should be able to handle the knowledge that you do have other clients, so if you know you'll be in a situation that could run interference with your work with them, manage their expectations.

> *"Mr. Horowitz, if you need to reach me Wednesday, it may be difficult. I'll be accompanying a client to surgery and they limit cell phone use in the hospital. But I will be checking messages as often I can, so if you need me, please know that I'll call you back as soon as possible."*

7. Encourage decision-making based on values and beliefs.

Beyond any major decisions they may need to make, there are other times your client should make decisions based on values or beliefs (religious or others). For example, a Jewish client may not wish to meet with you on a Saturday because it's his holy day. Or, if you are a female advocate, you may find some clients, based on their culture or just personal preference, would respond better to a colleague who is male – or vice versa.

The key here is to be supportive of these points of view. You might even ask about them, explaining that it's a learning experience for you.

8. Empower your clients.

Help your patients help themselves by teaching them and giving them tools. Help them look up terminology and medspeak. Help them create their own glossary. Teach them some anatomy as it relates to their medical challenges.[20] Show them how to find credible

---

20 If you use a smartphone, iPad or tablet, you can download any of a dozen anatomy apps to take to your next client meeting.

websites that aren't skewed by pharmaceutical company marketing tactics, or offered by quacks who will claim to cure their cancer in Nicaragua.[21]

9. Let clients determine pros and cons.

There will be times during your work with your clients that decisions will best be made by listing pros and cons.

But how can you know which ones will be considered pros by your client, and which ones will be considered cons?

The best answer is to let your client tell you which are which, and not to make assumptions yourself about which list they belong to. For example, you might assume that seeing a doctor in another city would be a con because of the travel involved, whereas your client may decide it's a pro because his favorite niece lives in that city and it will give him an opportunity to visit her.

10. Think outside the healthcare system box.

Those advocates who come to their new work from outside the healthcare system may have a leg-up on this one. It's about the forest and the trees.

Sometimes the best questions and answers result from thinking like an outsider. A nurse who has worked in the same hospital for decades, and understands the processes and protocols like the back of her hand, won't necessarily recognize when there may be a problem with one of those processes and protocols.

An enemy of advocacy is the suggestion that something is the right way to do it because "we've always done it that way before."

A patient is diagnosed with cancer and calls you to inquire about your help. "Can you help me sort through my treatment options?" he asks. One advocate will reply, "I'd be happy to help you with that." But the better advocate will reply, "Before we sort through those options, let's talk about getting a second opinion."

If you don't already have the ability to take two steps backward before you move forward, then work on it, and get good at it, and be sure that your client isn't being railroaded into something that may not be the right answer.

---

21 Find printable advice about website credibility in the Resources section in the back of this book.

11. Manage expectations for both the good and the bad.

I've preached throughout this book about managing expectations, but let's reiterate here that it's important to do so for both good and bad possibilities.

> *"Yes, Mrs. French, I was able to make an appointment for you with Dr. George." (That's the good news.) "Just so you know, though, the only appointment available was at 1:30, so you may miss your soap opera that day." (The bad news.)*

Problems anticipated don't take nearly the toll that unanticipated or unexpected problems do. Further, unexpected problems may be blamed on you – fair or unfair.

So to the extent possible, manage your client's expectations in all directions.

12. Don't Be Afraid to Say No

There are actually a couple of different ways "NO" comes into play.

Like the advocate previously mentioned, there are times when you will be asked to do things that aren't fair, or kosher, or legal – we've addressed those more closely in Chapter Ten.

Another "no" opportunity might occur when a client asks you to extend your services beyond your scope of work. We dealt with that in Chapter Eight. You are not expected to do anything at all that is outside your agreed scope of work, the tasks you're being paid for, so be sure you handle any such situation as professionally, but firmly as you can.

There's another "NO" to consider – that is – turning down a client or rejecting a contract before you even begin working together.

You are under no obligation to work with any client, or to perform any services you don't feel are part of your abilities or your wish to provide. You are under no obligation to work with any client for any reason at all. Period. Maybe it's just a sense you have, or maybe the person owes you money, or maybe another advocate has had a negative experience[22] but don't ever feel obligated.

If you don't want to work with someone, you can just tell them you're sorry, but you're too busy, then refer them to another advocate, or even send them to the AdvoConnection Directory.

But maybe you aren't sure. Maybe you're very busy, but for some reason you just don't want to turn them away with nothing but a "No." Maybe the client is a definite maybe.

---

22 This is a service provided by APHA. It helps advocates research potential clients who mention they have worked previously with another advocate, in case problems have arisen in that relationship.

In that case, here's an approach you can use which I have used a dozen times in my career.

If you aren't sure if you really want to work with a client, have your discussion about the scope of work. Then, without making any commitments, give them a price that is twice or more what you would ever charge for that type of work. If you'd charge a regular client $1500 – then tell this "not really sure" potential client that you would have to review it closely, but you think you'd charge somewhere around $3,000.

More than likely they will say "no thank you" – and that will be the end of the conversation. But you won't have rejected them. You're just too expensive for them.

But if they say yes? Well then – you'll be making twice what you expected and it will be worth any additional grief for working with them.

What about a client who you've contracted with, but find part way through the contract that you are in an impossible situation? It can happen, and it will probably be unpleasant. But if you find you are working with someone that difficult, then the sooner you cut off the relationship the happier you will be.

> *Mrs. Coughlin, I can see that we're having problems getting this work done. I feel as if you are putting roadblocks in my way, and I know you aren't satisfied with my work. I would like to terminate this contract. I will provide you with an accounting of what I have accomplished and will refund your money for the time I have not yet used. I think we'll both be happier that way.*

It's not easy, and it requires a tough skin. But some clients just aren't worth the grief. Better to cut your losses.

13. Limit Opportunities for Disagreement

As I've repeated often – at the time in their lives when patient-clients begin working with you, their lives are not going well. They are uncertain, and sometimes just plain scared. As a result, they may also be cranky, angry, frustrated and more.

Unless you know your patient-client very well, say because they are a relative or friend, or even attend the same church or synagogue as you, then this is not the time to discuss religion or politics or any of those topics that can become contentious. Expressing your opinion, which may not be the same as theirs, can put a wedge between you and your charge. That's not good for your relationship, and could even impact their health or progress.

Exceptions do exist; for example, if you attend the same church or synagogue, a discussion might be welcome. Or if your patient-client has already expressed a political viewpoint and you know the two of you see eye-to-eye, then just tread lightly.

The same advice holds true for being public about your opinions in general. While you may be a soapbox kind of person who loves nothing more than writing letters to the editor, or responding to blogs, if you are perceived by any of your target audiences as being argumentative, or even passionate about a cause, and your belief system conflicts with a potential client's belief system, then you run the risk of losing their possible business at a later date.

Steering clear of disagreements or arguments just makes good business sense.

Legal and Insurance Best Practices

1. Be a facilitator, not a decision-maker or recommender for your client.

There may be many times during your relationship with a client that she wants to lean on you to make decisions for her.

Don't.

For example, your client agrees that seeking a second opinion is a good step. So she asks you to recommend a doctor. Don't.

Another client is diagnosed with pre- diabetes and the doctor has provided two treatment options. You find a third and fourth, explain them to your client, and he asks you which of the four you would choose. Don't tell him. Deflect.

Or your client agrees that he will go with you to meet with hospital billing people, and he decides at the last minute that he doesn't want to accompany you. Plan to reschedule – because any settlement decisions will have to come from him anyway.

In all these cases, and hundreds of others, you need to make sure that your client is the one making the decisions, and that your client remembers he or she was the decision maker.

Why? To protect yourself.

If you are the one to make the decision, and something goes wrong, then you are culpable. For example, if you recommend a specific doctor, who then makes a mistake – then there is a good chance you'll be a part of any lawsuit that might get filed. At the very least, the client and his or her family will blame you – and talk about that to others.

The same is true for any sort of decision that will affect diagnosis, treatment or money. Just don't go there.

Here are some ways to be sure your client is the one making the decisions, and, just as important, is fully aware that he or she was the decision-maker.

First – as the great expectation manager you're becoming – tell your client in the early stages of your relationship that he or she will be responsible for all decision-making. Make it perfectly clear. Reiterate as often as needed.

Second – develop tools that help you help your clients. When a choice needs to be made from two or more options, like when choosing a new doctor, or the client's choice of treatments, then write them down and let your client circle his or her choice, then sign the paper. You can produce that before or after discussing pros and cons (see #9 in Customer Service Best Practices).

Some clients will be more insistent than others that you help them decide. But that's the key – HELP them, but don't decide. You can make the decision easier for them by helping them through the process, using explanations such as:

> *One of my clients found this doctor to be very difficult to understand, but she felt that in the end, he did the right things for her.*

Or

> *You know that if you don't make this decision, then it will be the same as choosing no treatment at all. Let's look at the possible consequences from that decision.*

Just be sure they know, in the end, that they were the ones who made the decision.

2. Never transport a client yourself.

Similar to making decisions for clients, transporting a client sets the stage for major problems, too. The moment your client falls, or is hurt getting in or out of your car, or you run late, making the client late, or any of a dozen other scenarios – you lose.

You aren't insured to transport them, which means you aren't insured if a problem arises.

Instead, help your client by making transportation arrangements with the local medical transport company, a cab company, or even your client's friendly neighbor. Then, if your work agreement calls for it, meet your client at the office, or hospital or whichever destination.

Yes – this approach is easier said than done. Many advocates have told me that's the expectation from (in particular) adult children of elderly parents who think that will be a part of the deal. Which is why you should consider adding a statement to your work agreement that states you will not be providing transportation. Then be sure to reiterate it during early conversations about the scope of work.

If a client or potential client gets upset that you are unwilling to be the driver, then you may be able to mitigate some of the upset. Explain that your insurance doesn't allow it. Further explain that it's not an efficient use of the time they are paying for. That your hourly cost is far higher than the medical transport company or cab driver's is.

3. Do not practice medicine.

Even if you are a clinical advocate, with years of nursing or doctoring under your belt, as an advocate, it is not your job to practice medicine. You are a facilitator, not a decision-maker or even a recommender. (See #1 in Legal Best Practices for more about this.)

If you are an advocate who does not have a clinical, practicing background, then this will be easy for you since you don't have the knowledge base to do so anyway.

But for advocates with clinical experience, this one is more difficult. You'll need to balance your license with your professional certifications with your insurance. There may be a few private advocates who can cross the line into practicing medicine, but only under certain circumstances, and often constrained by licenses, insurance, and state or provincial laws.

If you are tempted to practice medicine, then be sure you can do so without crossing any lines. Check with both your state or province licensing entity, your attorney, and your insurance broker, to see what they have to say.

By the way, this will also tie in to your client's expectations. If they have hired you as their advocate because they know you have a medical background, they will likely expect that's what you'll be doing for them—providing medical advice.

You'll need to explain to them clearly that as an advocate, that's not your role.

4. Be clear about who is performing which services.

I've listed this as a legal best practice, but it might have been listed in customer service, too; that is, making sure your client has a clear idea of who is who, and what their role is.

The best example, and perhaps your most frequent attention to this, will be any subcontractors who work with you. Even though you will have been clear in your contract that it might be a subcontractor who works with your new client, your new client may be surprised (and upset, even disturbed) when someone besides you takes over this or her case.

The same might be true when a transportation van arrives to take your client to a doctor's office, or if a home health company steps in to begin managing medications – whatever the different person's role, be sure your client knows who those people would be, and why they have the standing and expertise to help. Then use that information as a way to distinguish why you, the person they have already learned to trust, may not be the next person they work with.

To smooth these kinds of transitions, and unruffle any disheveled feathers, consider being there during the first meeting between the subcontractor and the client, even if it's only to make introductions.

5. Help your client prepare advance directives.

This is a great role for an advocate because it's a difficult conversation for families. Many older clients will embrace your willingness to help them with this task, because they find younger family members balk at discussing end of life issues with them.

The "right" documents to discuss, and the documentation of end of life decisions, vary from state to state and province to province.[23] Some recognize living wills, others do not. Most recognize DNRs, but they are documented differently. Then there are POLST and MOLST documents (Physician Orders or Medical Orders for Life Sustaining Treatment.) Notarization is required for some, and not for others. Laws vary from state to state or province to province.

Learn what documents are accepted and recognized in your client's state or province and if appropriate, offer this service to your clients and potential clients.

However! If your client asks you to be his or her medical proxy or, s the US Federal Government calls it, a "personal representative", you'll want to respectfully decline. This puts you into that role of making decisions on their behalf, and it's possible that neither your license (if you are a doctor or nurse), nor your insurance will cover you for such a position.

6. Don't request or accept compensation for referrals.

There are so many conflicts-of-interest within the healthcare system these days that we advocates need to stay above the fray on this point. Because the moment you request or accept compensation for making a referral, you have become a salesman, and have left advocacy behind.

Here's an example: There are hundreds of people who call themselves advocates who help families find the "right" nursing home or assisted living facility for elderly patients. These nursing home consultants will tell you they make recommendations based on the patient's needs and budget and whatever else they can claim to make it sound as if they are truly client-focused. Not only that, their service is free to the decision-maker.

Free? The magic word, of course.

Most don't disclose the fact that they are paid a nice fee or commission by the "right" facility. If we did a study of which placement was "right," it's entirely possible we would learn that it was more right for their wallets than it was for the patient.

That is the perfect example of a conflict-of-interest. It's a kick-back, a brokerage. Even if that salesman is pure of heart and only ever makes the "right" recommendation, the fact

---

23 Find more information for helping your clients with advance directives in the Resources section in the back of this book.

that anyone might question it brings it under scrutiny. It's the perception, even if it's not the reality.

Might you ever be in a situation that a referral fee or commission could be appropriate? Yes, it's possible. However, you'll want to ask yourself if the recommendation is being made for the client – or for you. This will be true for any recommendation or referral you might make, no matter how sincere you are that it's the right choice. And while, yes, you have to watch out for yourself, be sure the choice is being made to create a win-win scenario, and that it won't be perceived as anything but a decision being made in the best interest of your client.

7. Prepare to leave a client behind.

Some clients are more difficult to work with than others. And some are just impossible.

Advocates report clients who don't pay their bills, a client who refused to adhere to treatment recommendations (but blamed the advocate when his health didn't improve), abusive language, even a client who began stalking his advocate, including contacting a new advocate and telling stories about the former one that were not true.

There are many good reasons to "divorce" a client, whether or not yours is described above. The stress of a contentious relationship won't improve the health of either one of you. Only you will know whether terminating the relationship is the right choice for you.

The best practices associated with this eventuality are – first – to be sure you have a clause in your client contract that provides a process for terminating the relationship. (See Chapter Ten)

And second, to know that there are better ways to walk away than others, both legally and ethically. Simply failing to return phone calls or emails will not accomplish what you might hope it will, and could, instead, cause trouble for you down the road.

If you find yourself in a position of needing to terminate your relationship with a client one day, you'll want to be aware of any state laws that may apply according to your contract (another good reason to consult an attorney to develop your original contract). Then be sure you work out a process that you know leaves your client with all his/her records and the best taste possible in his or her mouth.[24]

8. Don't break the law.

OK – I see you rolling your eyes! A real "No, Duh!" moment. But there are two reasons I bring this up as a Best Practice.

---

24 A step-by-step process for ending a client contract is available through APHA.

First, because when people are desperate, they do desperate things that their non-desperate, thinking selves would never do. I see this every day when people make choices to undergo certain kinds of elective surgery despite overwhelming evidence toward the negative, or when they decide to eat some kind of wacko diet to cure their cancer instead of being treated in more conventional ways. (Not that I'm saying the conventional ways are always better – I'm not. Just that denial is never a good platform from which to make medical choices.)

Here's how this problem affects you. You'll have clients who will ask you to do things that, even if they aren't totally illegal, they will skirt the laws. You must say no to those requests because doing anything differently will put you and your practice in jeopardy.

Examples: You're working on negotiations with a hospital over a client's bill, and the client asks you to fudge on the numbers. Or a client who is terminal and in pain asks you to leave his entire bottle of oxycodone next to his bed.

Just don't.

Management Best Practices

1. Do a thorough assessment of your client and his or her needs as you begin your client relationship.

Whether you do this assessment before or after you enter your contract work with your client (See Chapter Eleven – Workflow), be sure you have all the background information you need to do your job.

There are two reasons to be so thorough.

First, because you can't possibly determine all the steps needed to perform your work without that complete background review. For example, if you are a med-nav advocate, then you may need a range of information from family history, to a current list of medications, to a past list of medications as they apply to current health status, to lists of all doctors and labs involved and more. If you don't have all that information, how will you coordinate it all?

Second, you'll need that thorough assessment to help you price your work. If you make a promise that you can complete a project for $1,500, covering 10 hours of work, only to learn there was an entire aspect of your client's situation that you knew nothing about, that perhaps they "assumed" you would just handle for them, then you'll be put in a difficult position – and you'll lose money.

You'll want to develop a worksheet that covers all aspects of the work someone could need to coordinate with the Care Plan template you'll develop.

It may take you awhile to get it right. Each client will have a unique situation and needs, but it's important you learn how to uncover all the possibilities early in your conversations.

2. Be clear with your client about what the goals of your work together are.

There will be nothing more disappointing or frustrating than finding out that your client thought you were aiming at one target, and you, the advocate were aiming at a different one.

Be very, very clear in your discussions with your client about what their outcomes can possibly be. Manage their expectations, and make sure they are dealing with reality. Clients may tend toward magical thinking, especially when they are sick, and if they feel desperate.

You may believe you were hired to accompany your client to doctors' appointments to be sure your client best understands the care he or she is getting and how to adhere to the doctor's recommendations (which, in the perfect world, have been agreed upon by the client.) In the same relationship, the client may believe that because she has hired you, she will be cured of whatever she's been diagnosed with. There is a wide, wide chasm between those two outcomes.

Much of this expectation management will come from disclaimers in your contract, and conversations you have. But be pro-active in discussing your goals and expectations throughout your relationship to be sure you are both still on the same plate, headed in the same direction.

A disconnect in these expectations could be devastating to you both.

3. Document, document, document, and write things down, too.

In Chapter Eleven – Workflow, we discussed the need to track your work, including the tasks you perform and your time.

One reason documentation is so important is because you'll always have at least two people you're tracking information and tasks for – your client and yourself. The minute you add a new client to your roster, you will have trouble remembering what you've done for whom – unless you keep track.

Another reason it's so important is because some time may pass between contacts with your client. With each passing hour, you have the opportunity to forget more.

Still another reason to document each step you take is so you can share that information with your client. Some advocates issue a weekly report to their clients. Others wait and provide the documentation with the final invoice. Still others provide the documentation along with any other records once a final payment has been made. (See Management Best Practices #8.)

The importance of good documentation can't be overemphasized. Good documentation can be a lifesaver – both figuratively and literally.

Consider the many aspects of your work you may document:

1. Document and track your time – the time of day and the time consumed.

2. Document every phone call and its results, which may include a recap of a conversation (see #3), the fact that you've left a message, or even a busy signal. If you need to follow up the call, make note of that, too.

3. Track every conversation you have in person, too: topics, decisions made, next steps, new questions to answer, whatever the conversation brings that you may need to refer to later.

4. If you do any kind of research on diagnoses, treatments, medical codes, or any other detail to benefit your client, be sure to track where you found the answers of interest.

5. Keep records including names and contact information for every person involved in your work with your patient, including family members, doctors, labs, hospitals, medical equipment, home health workers, and others.

6. Keep a calendar – one for each client, and a master calendar for you.

7. Track any money spent that a client will, according to your contract, reimburse you for. For example, you may pick up a prescription drug for him, or you may have to have copies made of his records, and he doesn't like digital files.

8. Track any resources you come across that you can use for another client. In addition to noting them in your current client's records, note them in a bigger resource list, too.

4. Be sure your subcontractors meet IRS or CRA guidelines.

When you need help, it's a huge relief to be able to rely on someone who has the required expertise, who you can trust to do the job as well as you would do it.

We've covered work with subcontractors in previous chapters, but there is one best practice to remind you of. That is, be sure the IRS or CRA agrees that your subcontractor is just that – and not an employee.

Both the IRS and CRA have specific guidelines to help you determine whether a worker is considered an employee vs a subcontractor. The rules do change on occasion. Be sure that in any given year, you don't run afoul of their parameters. They address everything from how the work is done, to when it is done, to what tools are used and more. Links to their current rules can be found in the Resources section at the back of this book.

5. Ask and Answer

Rare is the health advocate – or any professional, for that matter – who doesn't find himself in a circumstance that warrants asking for advice once in a while. Even if you know everything today, something will change tomorrow, and you'll need to tap into someone else's expertise to learn about it.

And vice-versa. You are the right person with the right answers some of the time. Others may reach out to you for advice or guidance.

Network with others – even your competitors. There are hundreds of people who would be happy to help you, or would be appreciative if you helped them. Participate in the various forums, conferences and other gatherings, online and in person. Join your local Chamber of Commerce or business networking group. Share your own knowledge with those who need assistance.

"Each one, teach one." It will help us grow this profession to the recognition and esteem it deserves.

Miscellaneous Best Practices

1. Stay safe.

Sadly, this needs to be mentioned among the best practices for health advocates. That is, that it's possible that not every potential client who contacts you for a meeting will do so with good intentions.

If you plan to meet with clients in their homes, consider whether or not you will be safe if you go there by yourself. News reports on occasion tell of real estate agents who have been robbed, or assaulted (or worse) when showing up at the request of someone who claimed they were interested in buying or selling a home.

For a first time meeting, if possible, meet in a public space, or in an office where there is more than just you. If you work from a home office, make plans to meet at a local coffee shop or lunch stop.

As you get to know your client better, you'll be able to assess your comfort level for meeting with him or her. Common sense can dictate.

But don't take risks based on a phone conversation with someone you don't know.

2. Learn to say "I don't know."

Nobody can ever know everything there is to know about everything at the very moment they need to know it. And that goes for you, too.

Further, no one expects anyone to know everything about everything. They don't expect that of you either.

If you are asked a question by a client or another professional, and you don't know the answer, or you know only part of the answer, then go ahead and admit you don't know or aren't sure....

Followed by a statement that explains that you'll either get the right answer, or you'll work with them to find the best answer; whatever is appropriate.

And add a time frame when it makes sense.

> *Mrs. Buchanan, I'm not sure how that will work, but I'll check in with Dr. French and I'll get back to you as soon as I get an answer from him or his nurse.*

Pretending to know something, or just as bad, fudging your way through something you aren't sure of, can come across as arrogant, and won't be useful. If the person you've answered finds out later you were wrong, then that can create real problems for you and your practice.

Admitting that you need to know more, and will take time to find an answer, comes across as credible, and makes you more trustworthy.

Which takes us to our last best practice...

3. Never stop learning.

All important professions encourage their practitioners to continually learn more and more about their craft. We expect no less from health advocates.

Just like the previous best practice called "Ask and Answer"; the way to grow your capabilities is continuous learning.

Opportunities range from weekend workshops, to certificate programs, from masters degrees to membership organizations. You'll find them in-person, online, even through teleconference call-ins on topics that will help you expand your practice and serve your clients.

A master list of learning opportunities can be found at www.HealthAdvocatePrograms.com.

Chapter Fourteen
Build Your Business Plan

That moment you've been dreading has arrived. You may my warning in Chapter Three that we would be tackling this eventually. Yes, now, in Chapter Fourteen.

But here's the good news. You've already done all the heavy lifting.

If you have followed along in this book, step by step, and if you have taken the time to handle the tasks in the workbook as you've gone along, then you have already created most of the necessary components, and have probably made most of the tough decisions, too.

Piece of cake.

Why Go to All That Trouble?

No matter how skilled a carpenter is with his saw or hammer, he needs to follow a plan or blue print as he constructs.

And so it is with a business. We need to know what it is we are trying to build, or we may end up wasting our time and money on building something we don't like, or that doesn't work.

But there are other reasons a business plan may be important, too:

1. **To raise money from other people or organizations.**
   Showing them how well you have thought through the many aspects of starting and growing your practice will give them confidence that you are serious about your goals, and know what it will take to reach them.

2. **To get support or buy-in from your family and friends.**
   In the perfect world, your family and friends would be supportive for no other reason than because you ask them, too. But a well-framed, written business plan, with its lists and charts and goals, will be highly impressive to them and will garner even stronger support.

3. **To boost your confidence.**
   I hope that as you have worked your way through this book, you've become more and more excited about launching this important new phase of your career and life. Attempting to take such a huge step without a plan in place would be overwhelmingly daunting. But with a plan in place, it's more like mildly nerve-wracking.

4. **To make sure your practice works toward your goals.**
   You may remember, way back in Chapter Three (and Task #3 in your workbook) that you worked on determining your goals. Including them in your business plan will help you continue working toward meeting them.

The Big "However"

The big "however" is simply recognition that there can be way too much emphasis on a business plan as a document. Some new business starters spend so much time trying to perfect their document that they lose sight of what they are really trying to accomplish which is, to open their doors and begin passing out their business cards.

Still others use their business plans as excuses. "I can't really start my business yet because my business plan isn't complete." Only sometimes it never does get finished, but is used as an excuse for years.

Still others believe their business plan must follow some sort of standard "official" format, as if the perfected format will be what makes it work.

But no – there is no official format. It doesn't have to be formal. And it's not meant to create an excuse.

Create What Works for You

A formal business plan, one that looks good on a shelf and makes a bank's loan officer salivate, must include plenty of verbiage and explanations like vision and mission statements, executive summaries and competitive analyses.

But in my (not so) humble opinion, unless you are composing your business plan to apply for bank funding (as opposed to Aunt Stella and Uncle Charlie), you can forget about all of those things.

If you want to be more thorough with your business plan, feel free to do so, of course. I've provided a handful of additional, excellent resources for writing formal business plans in the Resources section in the back of this book, ranging from forms you can fill out, to online courses offered (free!) for creating your business plan.

But there is no business that succeeded or failed based on its vision or mission statement or executive summary. And because health advocacy is so new, competitive analyses aren't worth their effort (At least not yet. If you are reading this in 2020 then by all means, you'd better do a competitive analysis.)

Important Business Plan Components for Health Advocates

These are the components you need to get your business started and your psyche prepared for hanging out your own shingle:

1. **Your story:** Why do you want to be a health advocate? Why do you want to help others weather or coordinate their journey through whatever aspects of the system you plan to help them with? What is your background, or even your backstory, that compels you to want to take this step? (We looked at this question in Chapter Three.)

2. **Your business description:** This is your elevator speech, the 30 second description of what your business is about, who your market is, and why it's a viable business idea. We tackled elevator pitches in Chapter Nine.

3. **Your goals and objectives:** Return to the questions you answered in Chapter Three which covers your goals. Knowing so much more now that you've read this far in this book, do you want to adjust them at all? What will your business look like in five years? In ten?

4. **Your marketing plan:** Who needs you? Why do they need you? What will compel them to hire you? How will you relieve their fear, uncertainty and doubt? What will you ask of them once you've completed your work (that is, besides compensation!)? We worked on your marketing plan in Chapter Nine.

5. **Business details:** What kinds of licensing do you need? What will your phone number be? What sorts of contracts will cover you and your advocate backside? What forms will you need? How will you track your clients so you don't get them mixed up? What insurance will you have in place in case a problem crops up? These are among the dozens of business questions you've already considered, some of which you have answered in many chapters in this book.

6. **Money details:** income, expenses, cash flow, Chapters Seven and Eight. Be capitalized and plan well.

TASK #16

Using the goals you determined in Chapter Three,
and the answers you've already developed throughout your
workbook, put together your Business Plan.

Voila! Your business plan is done.

Well. Kinda sorta.

A business plan is just that – a plan. Even though you begin by asking yourself the many questions your business will address, then answering them enough to give you the confidence to move forward, the truth is, a business plan is never really completed.

The best business plans are dynamic documents that update as business updates.

Those updates may be instigated by you; for example, if something isn't working well and you need to adjust, you'll want to adjust your business plan to accommodate for the change.

Or outside influences may require you to update your plan. For example, all advocates in private practice will need to adjust their plans if a national certification is developed, and based on that certification, states and provinces then decide to license advocates.

But for now, you've got what you need, and you've certainly got enough to get started.

I hope, that since you had already done such a thorough job with the tasks in earlier chapters in this book, that you feel as if developing your business plan was relatively easy – or at least easier than you thought it would be.

Chapter Fifteen
Throwing the Switch: Let's Get Started!

Y ou've done it!

You've made your way through (almost) this entire book. You have all the background knowledge to throw the switch and tell the world you ARE in business!

It's time to translate "all the background knowledge" into a checklist of pieces that need to be in place for you to actually accept a new client.

As an aside: please note that I said "actually accept a new client." Earlier, in Chapter Three, I answered the question about whether you should be telling the world that you're getting ready to open your practice. I suggested that it's a great running start on your marketing.

In this chapter, we're going to cross that line from "gonna be" to "am."

Accepting a new client means you're ready to hunker down and do the work with them that needs to be done. We walked through how that process works in Chapter Eleven (Managing Workflow). But even before that, you'll want to be sure the following pieces are in place:

- ✓ Your business plan should be completed so you have your roadmap.

- ✓ Your money should be available, liquid and ready for your expenses, as per the cash flow worksheet you developed.

- ✓ Your budget should be prepared so you can work within your budget limitations.

- ✓ Be sure you've got your business details covered – from your phone number to your professional email address. Begin answering the phone the way you planned in Chapter Eleven.

- ✓ Make sure your business bank account is ready to accept checks and pay bills.

✓   Your insurance needs to be active, ready to cover you from the moment your first client signs a contract.

✓   Your forms and contracts need to be prepared by, or approved by, your attorney, and ready to tailor for individual clients.

✓   Your marketing should be underway – from your own word of mouth, to the plans for a press release to send to local print publications about your new practice. Must haves include your business cards and a solid marketing-focused presence on the web.

✓   Join APHA as a Premium member (www.APHAdvocates.org) so that you are listed in the directory at www.AdvoConnection.com and potential clients can find you.

Now. It's time. THROW THAT SWITCH!

....

....

....

What? Can't do it? Are you stuck?

The Paralysis of Analysis

Some who read this book will be wonderfully prepared with that entire checklist, ready to start their practices, maybe with a few potential clients just waiting for them to be ready...

But some just won't do it. Something is stopping them. It's the paralysis of analysis.

It's the tendency to over think, to worry that something may not be right, or that they aren't really quite prepared, or that they'll make a mistake or that... that they aren't perfect...

.... Or that they will fail.

Not unlike a patient who can't make a decision about treatment, and therefore doesn't choose, and is therefore, defaulting to not being treated... an advocate who just won't throw that switch will forever be a "wanna be" – and will fulfill his or her own prophecy – failure by default.

My recommendation?

Either give up the idea right now, right this minute, and don't think about it anymore....

OR - Recognize that nobody is perfect, nobody launches their practice perfectly, and everybody makes mistakes.

Yes, everybody.

THEN - do something big to tell the world you are now officially in business. Send an email to everyone you know with an announcement (and of course, don't forget your call to action), or send postcards to everyone in your postal address book.

Or begin making phone calls to friends and acquaintances. Hang up posters at church or synagogue... Just do something that isn't difficult but results in you putting yourself on notice that there's no turning back.

Which now means that....

You are in business. Congratulations!

Please pause for a moment and take some pride in your accomplishment.

I, for one, am feeling a little like the momma bird who just kicked her baby from the nest.
I'm very proud of you.

Sure! Go ahead!
This is a blank page, and it's
your book, so make some notes...

Chapter Sixteen:
Your Success and the
Future of Health Advocacy

You are now an independent, private health advocate who runs his or her own practice, helping people weather their healthcare system problems every day.

Seriously – drink that in for a minute. The elation and the burden, too – but I promise you, there is much good to come!

How do I know?

For this final chapter, I've combined a bit of history with my crystal ball to manage your expectations, and predict the future, too.

The Future of Your Practice

A year from the date you open your doors, you will either be running a viable practice, or you won't.

Three years from now, you'll either be running a viable practice - or you won't.

Five, or ten, or 15 years from now, you'll either be running a viable practice, or you won't.

The future of your practice is actually quite black and white...

But the choices you make, for however long you choose to stay in business, will determine whether you end your business ownership successfully, or you close your doors because of problems. So perhaps that black and white is – really – plaid.

Your business journey in the first few years will be subject to a few "expectations":

Expectation #1:
If your business is like the thousands of other businesses that launch every year, it will take you three to five years to know if you'll be successful in meeting (or exceeding) your goals.

Actually, you will know much quicker than that if you aren't capitalized well (see Chapter Seven.) Bombing early due to under-capitalization is common.

But assuming you've capitalized your business and you're marketing yourself regularly, and on target, then you'll know in three to five years whether you're going to be as successful as you want to be.

Expectation #2:
You won't be an overnight success. It might appear that way to others, but "overnight" might actually last those three to five years mentioned in Expectation #1 before you feel as if you aren't putting in twelve hour days and seven day weeks.

Expectation #3:
In the early years, time flexibility is a myth. If someone tells me they started their own business because they wanted flexibility, I chuckle. Your flexibility might amount to choosing which 12 hours you'd like to work in any given day, or which day you'll take off this Fall. Once you make it through the first few years, then yes, you'll be able to take some time off, find folks to fill in for you, and more.

Expectation #4
...is actually an extension of #3. That is, that one of the most difficult things to achieve, especially in your first handful of years in business, is balance. Balance of work to play, personal life to work life, family time to work time and so forth.

Balance for a business owner isn't easy! So make it a goal. Plan to spend at least a few hours a day doing other things like taking a walk, going to the gym, reading to your kids, cooking a marvelous meal – whatever your fun is.

(By the way – I am absolutely the worst person to offer you advice about balance. Do as I say, and not as I do, OK? I truly do love my work, so my vocation and avocation don't have the same boundaries as many do, and as mine probably should.)

Expectation #5:
A partial solution to that lack of flexibility and finding balance is recognizing that you can't do everything yourself – and you shouldn't. As time goes on, you'll get better at

determining what you should, or shouldn't do for yourself. Examples: don't try to develop your own website if you haven't done so before, or don't try to create your own legal contracts unless you are a lawyer.

The key is to delegate. The earlier you learn to delegate to others, the sooner you'll be able to find balance and/or grow your expertise, too. Hire someone to help you with the aspects of your work you can't do, or don't have enough time to do, or you know are necessary but you really don't want to do yourself. Some advocates have hired virtual assistants to help them (see Chapter Five). Others hire marketing help in the form of graphic designers or web developers. Still others think "I can figure out how to do that myself" – but that's a problem because, unless the work they're talking about is their core business, then the learning curve will take them away from the billable hours needed to stay afloat.

Expectation #6:
You won't love (or even like) all your clients. In fact, you may find that some become downright abusive or belligerent. If you've prepared for difficult clients, meaning your contract provides a way to leave them behind (see Chapter Ten) and you've managed their expectations so they know what you're willing to tolerate, then this will be far easier.

But don't be surprised when you run into one of these PITAs (pains in the backsides). And you will run into them, I promise.

Expectation #7:
The opposite of the PITA's mentioned in Expectation #7 are the clients who will love you dearly. They'll love you so much that they will crave, crave, crave your attention, may become highly demanding, or even jealous if you spend too much time doing something other than helping them. Sadly, these folks will become PITAs, too, and you'll need to deal with them just the same way you deal with those described in Expectation #6.

Expectation #8:
Despite the "love" you'll get from most of your clients, you'll find that not all the other professionals you'll have to deal with will be so enamored. Advocates report resistance from doctors, hospitals and insurers who take umbrage at the advocate's participation, then erect barriers to make it more difficult.

However, as long as you have your paperwork and signatures in place, then you have the law – and fairness – on your side, too. Stay totally professional, don't lose your cool, treat them the way you'd want to be treated yourself, and keep your client aware of the resistance you're facing as you work through it.

The main point here is to not be surprised when it happens, because it happens to almost everyone. (If you run into continued resistance, it's a great conversation to have with other advocates who've already faced this demon.)

Expectation #9:
The flipside of dealing with those colleagues and professionals who may try to stymie your work, will be those who, once they have worked with you, or another client, will realize what a great resource you are for them, too.

Now that we are a handful of years into professional advocacy, I hear reports from those who have faced down the haters, and have turned them into supporters—even cheerleaders.

The advice is the same as in Expectation #8: stay professional, don't lose your cool, and treat them with respect. Once they realize that your work makes them look good, too, they'll be among your biggest fans.

Expectation #10:
In the first few years of being in practice, you'll find potential clients contacting you to help them with something you've not done before – a service that's not part of your core services.

You have your choice of whether or not you'll offer that service, and how you'll reply to the request, as we reviewed in Chapter Four. What I'm emphasizing here is how much the future of your practice will rest on the reply you provide.

For example: A new pizza shop opens, specializing in Hawaiian pizza (ham and pineapple toppings.) The first call-in order is for pepperoni and mushrooms – and the owner says "Sorry, we only offer Hawaiian pizza." The next call-in order is for mushrooms, onions and sausage, and the owner replies the same way. And so goes the next call-in, the next and the next.

What's going to happen to that pizza shop? His choices are 1. to adjust the menu, or 2. convince callers that what they REALLY want is Hawaiian pizza, or 3. to move his shop to an area that market research indicates truly loves Hawaiian pizza or 4. go out of business.

The lesson here is that your marketplace is going to determine your success. If all you are serving is Hawaiian pizza, you will likely go out of business. On the other hand, if you can either adjust your menu, or convince all your potential clients to give Hawaiian pizza-advocacy-services a try, OR – alternatively – to work hard at marketing yourself into your Hawaiian pizza niche, then you'll improve your chances of success.

Expectation #11:
You will make mistakes. You'll probably make lots of them.

I think it's this expectation that contributes to the paralysis of analysis we reviewed in Chapter Fifteen. If you fear those mistakes, then you may decide to forego pulling the trigger all together.

But if you know you'll make them – and expect to make them – and prepare ahead of time for when you do make them – then they won't sting in the same ways they will if you think you are perfect, or think you must be perfect to run a successful business.

The keys to mistake making are about fixing them afterwards. If they are business mistakes (math in a spreadsheet, or forgetting to pay the office rent), then they are easily fixable even if they are uncomfortable.

If they are advocacy mistakes, then the most important advice is to remain professional, apologize if need be, and if you can't figure out how to fix it yourself, then tap into the expertise of others who can advise you – lawyers, insurance brokers or other advocates.

As time goes on you'll grow a thicker skin, and you'll be able to tolerate your own mistakes more easily.

Just know that there is no escaping them. They are, after all, an expectation.

Expectation #12:
You will frequently find, no matter how experienced you are, that you'll be asked to do things you don't feel prepared for, but know you should understand. I'm not necessarily talking about new services here. I'm talking about things like understanding more about how the healthcare system in your area works, or expanding your cancer advocacy to other forms of cancer. They may be business things, or advocacy things, or anything in between. We took a look at this in the Gap Analysis chapter, Chapter Five.

Don't ever stop learning. The day you stop learning is the first day your advocacy practice will begin to fail. Not one of us can know everything, but we all have access to the resources that can help us cover the bases. Continuous learning is of fundamental importance to this profession; so much so, that it's one of the twelve professional standards.

Take classes, join advocacy and business organizations, read, debate – do what it takes to stay on top of your new profession.

Expectation #13:
Our final expectation is one you will experience frequently, but can't do anything about. That is – the world, and our professional environment will continually change.

The very forces that created the opportunity to establish and build this new profession of health advocacy will continue to shift the sands beneath us.

As long as you recognize that things will change, and expect them to change (no matter what they change to) then you'll be able to absorb them as needed. Remember back to Chapter Two where flexibility was highlighted as being crucial to your success? Now you better understand why that's true.

Many of those potential advocacy-sand-shifting forces are listed in the next section on the Future of Advocacy. But most of them aren't – because we have no idea what they will be.

One way to stay up with them, and overcome them when necessary, is to act on Expectation #11 – keep educating yourself.

And when you outgrow this book...

My hope for you would be that you outgrow the advice in this book in a very short period of time – within three years or less.

By "outgrow," I mean – that you will be ready to be bigger than this book. Throughout the book, for planning purposes, I've suggested you find subcontractors to help you, or that you expand your geographic reach when possible.

But suggestions, and the roadmap to do so, are two different things.

Just before you know you've outgrown this book, it will be time to tap into the expertise of those experts and professionals you'll find at the SBA, SCORE or your local SBDC. They'll help you assess what additional help you need, and they'll help you find it.

The Future of Health Advocacy

You've heard the saying, "The future's so bright, I gotta wear shades." One can't get much more optimistic than that.

There is some irony in the fact that it's entirely true for the future of health advocacy.

Follow along with me for a moment:

The capabilities of any healthcare system to serve its patients are growing exponentially through the use of technology and the speed-of-light ability to gain access to the knowledge needed to make it work. For example, a generation ago there was no cure for cancer. Today, for some cancers, a cure is entirely possible. We can only imagine tomorrow's possibilities.

As a result, people are living longer with a better quality of life for that "extra" time they might not otherwise have enjoyed. Instead of dying younger from a disease that couldn't be controlled, they are now being cured, or at least managing those diseases, then living longer – long enough to acquire new diseases that need curing or managing - diseases they never would have developed if they had died young. Or, as stated in the Introduction to this book, the 75-year-old who didn't die of a heart attack at the age of 50 has now lived long enough to develop diabetes and prostate cancer. Some estimates say that 17 percent of people who live to 75 will also live to age 100.

That longer, higher-quality life requires much more in health system resources, and squeezes the resources that do exist. Further, the healthcare-seeking population continues to expand because those who might have dropped out (died early), haven't. For example, it's more difficult to get an appointment with one's doctor, or to get a test or treatment approved by insurance, or to find a new liver for a transplant candidate, because there are so many others who want/need/have a right to them, too.

That combination of longer-living people and squeezed resources is what creates the challenges our potential clients face – they are competing for the care they need.

That's precisely what has created a void – and the opportunity for us health advocates.

Or, put more succinctly – our opportunities for success exist because the healthcare system can't support its own success.

We covered all the reasons this is THE TIME for health advocates in the Introduction to this book. From aging baby boomers, to our mobile society, from outside responsibilities to the lack of enough providers, and from too many medical errors to the growth of technology – even healthcare reform in the United States – we are on our way to the tipping point of need, and you have wisely decided to ride that wave.

But just as we recognize the need for advocacy services, it's wise to look forward to the influences that may mean less of a need, or may mean the need changes or shifts, or even those things that may come down the pike to influence our work, or how we do our work in the future.

So here's an attempt to identify what some of those influences might be.

Certification and Licensing

As stated earlier, private, independent advocacy and navigation are so new, that no nationally recognized credential exists to provide a set of standards or expectations for what someone can expect if they hire a private advocate.

But someday that national standard will exist, and it's entirely possible that provinces and states will begin to license advocates someday, too. It's probably safe to assume that once certification requirements are established, grandfather clauses will allow those who have already developed a respected track record to be certified without having to fulfill their other, possibly more rigorous requirements.

Future certification requirements are good reasons to get started in your practice sooner rather than later. But keep your eyes and ears open for changes in this area, too. This is one reason it's vital you participate in one or more professional advocacy organizations. They'll keep you updated on any progress in certification or licensing.

Large Advocacy Companies and Franchising

A small handful of large companies already exist that provide advocacy services mostly to large corporations that insure themselves and are looking for ways to save money on their overall healthcare expenditures for their employees.

But the future of advocacy will be to offer services to individuals, and branding those services nationwide. The entire concept will become better known, which is great news for you, the individual advocate. You'll be able to focus your marketing efforts on your individual practice instead of trying to educate the population at large.

There are fewer than a half-dozen of these companies already in existence, either working with individual advocates as subcontractors, or franchising their operations in different parts of the United States. Look for more of them to pop up within the next ten years.

The Aging Population

Yes, we have the baby boomers to thank for a good advocacy karma. The older population is our largest target audience and will keep us in good advocacy work for the next couple of decades.

But what happens in 20 years when the pool of baby boomers begins its big decline? That decline will have an impact on our total pool of potential clients.

For now, and probably for the next 12-15 years, this isn't a concern except as it may influence how you go out of business. You may choose to sell your business in 10 years, or expand your services to accommodate for a smaller elderly population.

Keep obsolescence in mind so you don't end up like Kodak, Britannica or Smith Corona. (Remember them?)

Medical Tourism

According to the cliché, the world is getting smaller. Communications makes it so, including the easy, affordable and vast access we all have to the Internet and its knowledgebase.

That means that patients no longer confine themselves to their own geographic space for the care they seek, at the price they are willing to pay.

Today this effect is most pronounced for many elective procedures patients choose. If I can get my tummy tucked for half the price, and vacation in Singapore at the same time – well – why not?

Unless some unforeseen (probably political) force comes about to change this tourism momentum, we will likely see more and more patients travel from one state or province to another, or from one country to another to get their choices of medical services. Instead of being upset that their insurance doesn't cover a test or procedure, or isn't offered locally, they will instead buy a plane ticket.

To the extent this geographic freedom may influence your practice as time goes on, you'll want to either embrace it, or learn to work around it.

Follow the Money

As healthcare dollars are squeezed tighter and tighter, whether those squeezers are private insurers or governments, patients react to that squeeze by looking for alternatives.

The squeezed dollar, whether it's being squeezed to make money or save money, results in rationing, and no one wants to think they can't get a diagnosis, test or treatment they need because their care is being rationed.

The money squeeze is affected by all the situations listed here and is, perhaps, the one aspect of advocacy and healthcare delivery that (probably) won't change. It may look different (squeezing may take place in different ways by different groups) but in the long run, money, the very problem that has the biggest negative effect on today's healthcare delivery, will be the one that has the biggest effect decades from now, too.

Awareness and Empowerment

Patients and their caregivers are becoming savvier than ever. A generation of well-educated, curious baby boomers are spending more and more time delving into every piece of information they can find to educate themselves about their health challenges. The generations behind them will follow in their footsteps, most assuredly with better tools and certainly with access to far more medical research results and discoveries.

The more they learn, the more they are exposed to the negatives of the healthcare system, too; medical errors, conflicts-of-interest, all those aspects of the system that stand between them and the effective care they deserve.

The more these "e-patients" (empowered, equipped, enabled) know, the more they will understand the need for a professional advocate by their side.

Finally - specifically in the United States:

Healthcare Reform and Insurance

What kind of influence will healthcare reform and the tightening of the insurance dollar have on those in the US who establish private advocacy practices? Well, let's just say that for now, I call them "job security."

The more confused and upset patients are, the more likely they will be to turn to a private advocate.

My timeline guesstimate for riding this wave is 12-15 years. Because healthcare reform is so highly politicized, and because there are bound to be unintended consequences, it's impossible to predict (my crystal ball isn't nearly clear enough!) but there will at least come a time when we are no longer confused. The lack of confusion may result in a situation Americans are happy to embrace (not likely) or it may mean even more work for advocates who will be hired by those who aren't happy and know even more clearly that they need someone to help them.

Some Final Words

One of my favorite quotations is this:

Luck is the point at which preparation meets opportunity.[25]

I'm a believer. And I also believe that you, now the well-prepared advocate and practice owner, are one very lucky person.

---

25 Although many people are credited with this quotation, the earliest seems to be Seneca, a Roman dramatist, philosopher, & politician (5 BC - 65 AD)

Resources

Find additional resources by chapters here.

If you prefer to link to web resources directly (rather than inputting this text), you can find them hotlinked from the book's website: **HealthAdvocateResources.com**

General Resources

The Alliance of Professional Health Advocates (APHA)	Free trial membership - details on page 211 or at: www.APHAdvocates.org/freetrial

---

Introduction

List of companies hiring advocates and subcontractors:	http://bit.ly/advocatejobs
Link to the workbook that accompanies this Handbook:	www.HealthAdvocateResources.com

---

Chapter Two—Skills for Running a Successful Practice

To help you understand the healthcare system in the US: You Bet Your Life! The 10 Mistakes Every Patient Makes (How to Fix Them to Get the Healthcare You Deserve)	The book's website: www.YouBetYourLifeBooks.com Or purchase at Amazon: http://amzn.to/YouBetYourLife
The Health Advocate's Marketing Handbooks	The book's website: http://HealthAdvocateResources.com/HABMH http://HealthAdvocateResources.com/AMH Or purchase at Amazon: http://amzn.to/AdvocateMarketing

Chapter Four—What Services Will You Offer?

Master list of current advocacy services being offer to patients and caregivers. This list is updated occasionally.

www.AdvoConnection.com/services.htm

If you offer a service not listed, please let us know and we'll add it to the list. (resources@aphadvocates.org)

Market Research—more information and links to resources:

Quickfacts from the US Census Bureau:
   http://quickfacts.census.gov/qfd/

From Entrepreneur Magazine:
   http://www.entrepreneur.com/
   article/217345

From Inc.com
   http://www.inc.com/guides/
   marketing/24018.html

From About.com Small Business Canada
   http://sbinfocanada.about.com/cs/marketing/a/
   marketresearch.htm

From the SBA (Small Business Administration)
   http://www.sba.gov/content/do-your-
   market-research

Chapter Five—Filling Your Education and Skills Gap

Education, Organization and Networking Resources for Health Advocates and those who wish to become advocates:

www.HealthAdvocatePrograms.com

Virtual assistants provide administrative help on a full or part-time basis.

Find lists of virtual assistants:

www.assistantmatch.com/

www.virtualassistants.com/

www.speakernetnews.com/post/
vawebmaint.html

Chapter Six—Business Brass Tacks

Small business advisors can be found at:

SBA—Small Business Administration (US)	www.sba.gov
SCORE (Service Corps Retired Executives)	www.score.org
SBDC (Small Business Development)	www.asbdc-us.org
CBN (Canada Business Network)	www.canadabusiness.ca/eng/

Corporation (incorporate) service:	www.corpnet.com

List of licenses you may need:	www.sba.gov/licenses-and-permits

Places to test your URL (web address) as you name your business:	www.godaddy.com www.register.com www.networksolutions.com

Employee vs. Subcontractor rules:

From the IRS	http://www.irs.gov/businesses/small/article/0,,id=99921,00.html
From the CRA	http://www.cra-arc.gc.ca/E/pub/tg/rc4110/rc4110-e.html

DUNS number (if you decide to apply for grants)	http://fedgov.dnb.com/webform/pages/CCRSearch.jsp

Online forums of interest to advocates:	The Alliance of Professional Health Advocates forum is open to members only. Log on to your membership dashboard and find the link.

Additional forums are located at Linked In:
(require membership at LinkedIn)
	www.LinkedIn.com look for:
	  Patient Navigator
	  Patient Advocates
	  Nurse Entrepreneurs
	  Society for Participatory Medicine

Find more Chapter Six resources on the next page: —>

Chapter Six *(cont.)*

Choose and use a professional communications service.

Email:
www.gmail.com
www.mail.com
www.hotmail.com

Use your own web address for your email.

Fax services:
www.efax.com
www.faxzero.com
www.popfax.com
www.extremefax.com

Toll free number and voice mail services:
www.evoice.com
www.google.com/voice
www.voicenation.com
www.ringcentral.com

Chapter Seven—Expenses and Funding

Use your website and/or smartphone to accept credit cards
www.Square.com
www.Paypal.com
www.Intuit.com

Cashflow basics from Entrepreneur Magazine:
www.entrepreneur.com/article/223288

Chapter Nine—Marketing Your Services

Directory listed members (www.AdvoConnection.com) can ask clients to add testimonials or endorsements to their listings at no charge.
www.advoconnection.com/submittestimonial.htm

Find a sample press release:
HealthAdvocateMarketing.com/downloads/PressReleaseFormat.pdf

Chapter Ten—Legal and Insurance

HIPAA and privacy:	Find an authorization for release of records in the Resources for this book at http://healthadvocateresources.com/SGOP/index.htm
Privacy laws in Canada:	Are overseen by the Office of the Privacy Commissioner. Information found at: www.priv.gc.ca/index_e.asp
Electronic signatures and privacy:	www.echosign.com www.docusign.com www.rightsignature.com
Secure email:	Thunderbird uses Enigmail (must be obtained through Mozilla.org) www.sendinc.com www.hushmail.com AppleMail can use an add on from GPG tools: www.gpgtools.org
Legal documents and forms (general) are found at:	www.docracy.com (free) www.LegalZoom.com (paid) www.DocStoc.com (paid)
BOP insurance information:	www.entrepreneur.com/article/52882
Incorporation:	www.CorpNet.com

Chapter Eleven—Managing Workflow

Sample Invoice:	Find a sample linked from the Resources at http://healthadvocateresources.com/SGOP/index.htm
Additional forms and contracts available to members of APHA: (Not all contracts and forms are available to all members. PACE members have limited access.)	Sample consultation agreement (advocate and client) HIPAA privacy forms Independent contractor working agreement Independent contractor non-compete agreement
Encrypted email or document signatures:	See Resources for Chapter Ten
Client tracking software and applications:	Navigation Tracker www.navigationtracker.com Jewel Code www.jewelcode.com Care Manager Pro www.caremanagerpro.com

Chapter Thirteen—Best Practices

To add to best practices, please send an email to:	resources@APHAdvocates.org
Print these guidelines for finding credible health information on the web:	http://patients.about.com/od/researchandresources/a/internetcred.htm
Advance Directives documents:	http://bit.ly/advdirectives
Determining status as employee or subcontractor:	See Resources for Chapter Six

Chapter Fourteen—Building Your Business Plan

Additional resources for understanding and building business plans:

From Entrepreneur Magazine:

www.entrepreneur.com/businessplan/index.html

From the SBA:

www.sba.gov/content/business-plan-executive-summary

Free online course from the SBA:

http://web.sba.gov/sbtn/registration/index.cfm?CourseId=27

Add your own resources here:

About the Author

When Trisha Torrey was diagnosed with a rare, aggressive lymphoma in 2004, she was a marketing consultant who knew almost nothing about healthcare. She was also naïve to the dysfunction of the American healthcare system that was tasked with treating her.

But she got smart, fast. She learned that the possibility of excellent care was too easily and frequently eclipsed by miscommunication and mistakes. She also learned that if she didn't stick up for herself, and insist on the help she needed, she would not get it. The more empowered she became, the more she realized there was a possibility she had no lymphoma. Eventually she proved she was right; she had no cancer.

Once Trisha put that noncancer odyssey behind her, she decided it was up to her to apply her skills to teaching others how to navigate the dangerous landscape of American healthcare. She sold her marketing company in 2006 to devote herself full time to the cause.

Today Trisha calls herself "Every Patient's Advocate." She is the founder of The Alliance of Professional Health Advocates (www.APHAdvocates.org) which supports the business aspects of a health advocate's work, and AdvoConnection.com which helps patients and caregivers find the help they need. She is the author of six books, all written to support patients and those who help them.

Trisha has appeared on CNN and MSNBC, and has been quoted by the Wall Street Journal, O Magazine, U.S. News and World Report, NPR, Scientific American, Health Magazine, Money Magazine, Angie's List Magazine, Bottom Line Publications, and others.

She lives in Central New York State with her husband, Butch, and her mini-mutt, Crosby. When she's not doing her patient advocacy thing, she enjoys playing golf, gardening, and working in stained glass.

She can be reached at trisha@diagKNOWsis.com or at any of the following:

Twitter: @TrishaTorrey
LinkedIn: www.LinkedIn.com/TrishaTorrey
Google+: gplus.to/trishatorrey
Facebook: www.facebook.com/EveryPatientsAdvocate
Facebook: www.facebook.com/AdvoConnection

diagKNOWsis™

About DiagKNOWsis Media

*DiagKNOWsis Media is the umbrella formation for all
patient and advocate activities developed by
Trisha Torrey since 2004. It includes:*

AdvoConnection for Patients
www.AdvoConnection.com

A website that helps patients and caregivers search for a
professional advocate. Those advocates are members of:

The Alliance of Professional Health Advocates
APHAdvocates.org

Provides private, independent health advocates with business
support. Benefits include access to advisors such as legal,
insurance, marketing, medical, patient safety and shared decision
making.

The APHA also sponsors the following sites:

Our Blog: www.APHAblog.com
Education: www.HealthAdvocatePrograms.com
Code of Ethics: www.HealthAdvocateCode.org
Practice Resources: www.HealthAdvocateResources.com

APHA Trial Membership Offer!

If you have purchased this book in either
print or e-book form, I invite you to become
a trial PACE member of The Alliance of Professional
Health Advocates for one month—for free!

A PACE membership helps you determine whether you
want to take the plunge to become a private, independent
advocate, then provides you with the tools and support to do so.

**To take advantage of this free trial offer, link to:
www.APHAdvocates.org/freetrial**

The instructions you need, and the rules for participation, are
found at that page.

We look forward to your participation in The Alliance of
Professional Health Advocates!

Every Patient's Advocate
www.EveryPatientsAdvocate.com
And blog, located at: www.EveryPatientsAdvocate.com/blog
Trisha's patient empowerment tips. Sign up to receive twice monthly emails with ideas for improving your journey through the healthcare system.

You Bet Your Life!
The 10 Mistakes Every Patient Makes (How to Fix Them to Get the Health Care You Deserve)
www.YouBetYourLifeBooks.com
Trisha's first book helps patients, caregivers and advocates better understand the healthcare system and point of view, then uses that understanding to provide tools and tactics to help them improve their medical system outcomes. Available from the books' website, or through online retailers (Amazon, BN) Bulk pricing is available.

Healthcare Speaker Available
www.HealthcareSpeaker.org
Trisha is available for speaking to many audiences about improving their interface with the healthcare system, from patients and caregivers to advocates, doctors, nurses and other healthcare professionals.

Bad Doctors in the News
www.baddoctorsnews.com
Provides information for people who are researching possible doctors, highlighting news stories about doctors who have been arrested, incarcerated, have had their licenses removed and more.

DiagKNOWsis
www.diagknowsis.org/homepage
Trisha's original website, developed after her cancer misdiagnosis, is comprised of resources that help patients, caregivers and advocates research a diagnosis, treatment options, professionals, quality and more.

DiagKNOWsis Media
www.diagKNOWsis.com
This is the main website for DiagKNOWsis media and provides a listing of all DiagKNOWsis activities.

The Health Advocacy Career Series

Find all these books linked from:
http://HealthAdvocateResources.com

1. **So You Want to Be a Patient Advocate?**
   Choosing a Career in Health or Patient Advocacy
   Do you have the knowledge and experience to either get a job or start your own practice? How much money can you make? What is the Allegiance Factor and how can it affect your work and your job satisfaction?

2. **The Health Advocate's Start and Grow Your Own Practice Handbook** (the book you are reading now)

3. **The Health Advocate's Basic Marketing Handbook**
   Makes marketing your advocacy services far easier than you might imagine. Includes all the basics: planning, target audiences, messaging, branding, advertising, public relations, branding and more.

4. **The Health Advocate's Advanced Marketing Handbook**
   Expands upon the Basic Handbook, including advanced branding, becoming an expert, developing your niche, public speaking, email newsletters and more.

5. **The Health Advocate's Low and No Cost Marketing Ideas Handbook**
   Contents as titled. To be published late 2015.

To be published in late 2015:

The Health Advocate's Low & No Cost Marketing Ideas Handbook

The Health Advocate's
Start and Grow Your Own Practice Handbook

Index

Index (cont.)

Index (cont.)

CPSIA information can be obtained
at www.ICGtesting.com
Printed in the USA
LVOW09s1046120617
537813LV00001B/2/P